Thank You, Lord

My "Thank You" Hits Different When You Know What I've Survived

Pastor Paul Steven Smith

KG
KAMB
PUBLISHING
GROUP

Kamb Publishing Group

Dedication

To every survivor who kept walking with scraped knees and a trembling heart. I dedicate this to all the wounded warriors who have learned to express their gratitude with tears in their eyes. To every person who thought they were not going to make it but DID. This one is for you.

And to my parents, Yvonne Liverpool Smith and Billy Hugh Smith, Sr., I am still carrying your strength. I am still standing because you both prayed, pushed, protected, and poured into me. Everything good in me has your fingerprints on it.

Brenda and Russel Payne, thank you for your love and support. You have been my greatest cheerleaders and motivators, encouraging me to finish the books. For that, I am truly thankful.

And to every soul God kept alive on purpose: We made it.

Special Dedication

To You, the one holding this book. Let me look you dead in your spirit and say this with my whole chest: Thank you.

Not the cute thank-you. Not the customer service thank-you. Not the "thanks for coming to my TED Talk" thank-you. No. I am thanking you with the kind of gratitude that comes from somebody who knows what it feels like to be scared to write, scared to be seen, scared to be judged, scared to fail, and still showed up anyway, only to discover you were waiting for me.

This book exists because you kept reading, kept supporting, kept listening, kept coming back, and kept believing in me before I fully believed in myself. You did not have to pick up this book. But something in your soul whispered, "This one is for you." And I do not take that lightly.

So, this page, this whole project, is dedicated to every survivor, every fighter, every broken-but-still-trying heart, every tired soul looking for hope, every person who almost gave up, every one of you who pushed through pain to grow anyway.

I wrote this book with tears, testimony, and truth, but YOU are the reason I released it. May these words heal you, lift you, strengthen you, confront you, encourage you, and wrap you in the same grace that wrapped me.

Thank you for trusting me with your journey. Thank you for letting me walk with you. Thank you for giving this little church boy from D.C. the honor of speaking into your life.

This book belongs to you now. Treat it like a survival kit. Treat it like a praise report. Treat it like a reminder: You are still here, and God is not done.

With love, laughter, and Holy Ghost power,

— Pastor Paul

About This Book
"Why I Had To Write This

This book was born in the middle of a storm. Not a cute storm. Not a drizzle. Not the "grab your umbrella and keep walking" kind of storm. I am talking about the kind of storm that makes you question your calling, your sanity, your stamina, your future, your faith, and even your Wi-Fi connection.

For years, I lived inside fear, pain, grief, and pressure that did not just beat me up. It tried to bury me alive. I survived moments that should have taken me out, seasons that broke other people, attacks that left me confused, and delays that made me wonder if I even mattered anymore.

But God kept me. Kept my mind. Kept my soul. Kept my breath. Kept my story going.

This book is my thank-you. Every chapter is handwritten in survival ink. Every page is dipped in gratitude, truth, laughter, and Holy Ghost fire. Every story is a piece of the journey I had to live so someone else could be set free.

This book is not designed to impress you. It is designed to heal you. It is for the tired. For the broken. For the almost-did-not-make-it. For the folks who have been carrying burdens in silence. For the ones who love God but still wrestle with life.

If you have ever lived through pain that did not announce itself, storms that did not give warning, tests you did not sign up for, or seasons you did not think you would survive, this book is designed for you.

Open it with expectation. Read it with honesty. Let it speak to your bones. And wherever you see yourself on these pages, know you are not alone, and you are not done.

Acknowledgments

L et me tell you something. Nobody survives life alone.

Thank you to the doctors, nurses, and radiation techs at Johns Hopkins who cared for me during my prostate cancer journey and treated me like a soul, not a statistic.

Thank you to Donald, my brother in the fight, who showed me what mutual encouragement looks like when two men are walking through fire but refusing to burn.

Thank you to Jo, the medical tech with 30 years of compassion, who made the hardest days feel lighter.

Thank you to every member of Victory Fellowship Church who stood beside me, prayed for me, supported me, and let me be both pastor and human at the same time.

And thank YOU, the reader, for trusting me with your heart, your story, and your healing.

How To Read This Book

- Read with an open heart.

- Pause when something hits your spirit.

- Journal after each chapter if you can.

- Highlight anything that feels like it was written specifically for you.

- Share your breakthroughs with someone who loves you.

- Be gentle with yourself.

- This book may touch places you have been avoiding.

Foreword

I f you are holding this book in your hands, let me warn you right now. This is not some cute little devotional. This is not the book you read while sipping chamomile tea with your pinky up. This is a surgery book. A testimony book. A Holy Ghost CPR book.

Because real deliverance does not come dressed in calm music and candlelight. It comes with sweat, tears, scars, flashbacks, breakthroughs, and a whole lot of "LORD, YOU BETTER COME GET ME TODAY."

This book is living proof that God still saves, still delivers, still restores, still heals, still interrupts funerals, still rewrites stories, and still pulls people back from the edge when the world has no clue.

And every chapter in here? It is not a theory. It is not philosophy. It is not research. It is my blood. My truth. My scars. My testimony. My survival.

So, take a breath. Open your heart. Sit down, if you need to. Stand up if the spirit hits you. Shout if the fire catches you. But whatever you do, do not treat this book like entertainment. Treat it like deliverance on paper. Because that is exactly what it is.

— Pastor Paul

Publisher's Notes

KAMB Publishing Group is honored to present this project from Pastor Paul Steven Smith, whose voice has become one of the most honest, bold, and transformational forces in inspirational literature today.

This book is more than pages. It is a testimony, a healing tool, and a survival manual for anyone who has ever faced fear, suffering, delay, heartbreak, uncertainty, or spiritual exhaustion.

Pastor Paul writes with a rare blend of vulnerability, humor, cultural truth-telling, and faith-filled fire that speaks directly to the hearts of everyday people, and this book continues that legacy. It reflects a lifetime of wisdom, lived trauma, divine intervention, and grace that refuses to let go.

At KAMB Publishing, we believe stories like this must be told, shared, and preserved, because they not only change lives, they save them.

We extend our heartfelt gratitude to each reader: Thank you for choosing this book. Thank you for investing in your own healing. Thank you for supporting independent Black authors and storytellers. May these pages remind you that your life matters, your story matters, and your survival is not accidental. It is intentional, purposeful, and sacred.

With gratitude,

KAMB Publishing Group

Washington, D.C.

Contents

Introduction
Why My 'Thank You' Is Not Regular

L et me tell you something before we go any further. This book you are holding? It is not just a book. It is not a cute memoir. It is not a simple testimony. It is not a feel-good devotional you skim through while waiting for your coffee. No.

This right here? This is my survival report. My praise report. My I-should-have-been-dead-but-God-snatched-me-back report. My "if you only knew what I fought through just to stay alive" report. This is the truth behind why my "THANK YOU, LORD" hits different.

Because I did not learn gratitude from a sermon, I did not learn gratitude from a conference. I did not learn gratitude from somebody's Facebook reel or a motivational quote. I learned gratitude the hard way. The painful way. The lonely way. The bleed-in-silence way. The cry-in-the-bathroom way. The hold-yourself-together-because-nobody-realizes-you-are-breaking way.

I learned gratitude in the dark. And when you have been kept in the dark, when God pulled you out of pits nobody saw, storms nobody knew you were drowning in, fights nobody knew you were losing, and grief nobody knew you were carrying, you do NOT praise God, cute. You cannot. Your "thank you" comes from another dimension. It comes from your bones. It comes from the part of your soul that almost did not make it home. It comes from the version of you that God resurrected while everybody else thought you were fine.

See, people see the me that laughs, writes, preaches, sings, encourages, and teaches. But they do not always see the me that survived sickness that tried to steal my hope, grief that knocked the wind out of me, depression that tried to take my life quietly, fear that almost robbed me of my calling, shame that tried to cover my future, mistakes that wanted to bury me alive, heartbreak that left cracks only God could fill, pain I did not deserve, trauma I never told, nights that lasted way too long, battles I fought with nobody praying for me but me, and seasons where all I had left was God's mercy holding me together.

And yet, here I am. Still breathing. Still standing. Still fighting. Still becoming. Still learning. Still rising. Still alive. And that alone deserves praise.

See, this book is not written by a man who had it easy. It is written by a man who had to praise his way through hell's waiting room. A man who had to survive himself, his fears, his doubts, his mistakes, his trauma, his past, his pain, his pressure, and his perfectionism. A man who had to tell the truth: "I did not keep myself alive. God kept me. Period."

That is why my "Thank You, Lord" hits different. It is not polite. It is not predictable. It is not rehearsed. It is not religious. It is raw. It is rugged. It is loud. It is lived. It is from the pit I climbed out of. It is from the storm I survived. It is from the night God held me together with nothing but grace.

This book is for anybody who has ever survived something they never said out loud. Anybody who has ever cried themselves to sleep. Anybody who has ever smiled while dying inside. Anybody who looked strong on the outside but was fighting for their life on the inside.

Is that you? Welcome. You are in the right place.

This book is my testimony. But it is also your permission slip. Permission to heal. Permission to feel. Permission to praise God without apology. Permission to say "Thank You, Lord" loud and unfiltered, because you survived things people do not even know about.

So, come on in. Turn the page. Let us walk through this thing together. And when you are done reading, if your "Thank You" is not louder, deeper, richer, stronger, and more unapologetic, I did not write this right.

But I believe you are about to finish this book with a praise that makes the angels look at each other like, "Yep, that one survived something."

Let us begin. Because my "Thank You, Lord" hits different.

— **Pastor Paul**

Chapter 1

My First Words Were Thank You Because I Shouldn't Be Here

But Mercy Stepped In

S CRIPTURE

Psalm 107:1-2 (KJV): "O give thanks unto the LORD, for he is good: for his mercy endureth for ever. Let the redeemed of the LORD say so, whom he hath redeemed from the hand of the enemy."

Psalm 107:1-2 (PASTOR PAUL'S Translation): "Listen here, somebody better open their mouth and thank God right now because His goodness does not have an expiration date and His mercy does not run out. And if He pulled you out of something that should have destroyed you, you'd better tell somebody about it. You'd better say so. You'd better testify.

You'd better let the world know that the enemy had you, but God snatched you back."

(The organ rumbles like thunder warming up.)

Let me tell you something right off the top, and I need you to hear me clearly because this is not a regular chapter. This is not some cute little "welcome to my book" introduction where I ease you in gently with soft music and dim lighting. No, sir. No, ma'am. This is a full-blown sanctuary moment. This is an opening-night revival. This is a call to order with a side of Holy Ghost oxygen. This is Pastor Paul stomping, Pastor Paul testifying, and Pastor Paul laying hands on the atmosphere before we even get to the first page of the real story.

I am talking about the kind of opening that makes the church mothers pull a peppermint out of their purse, look at each other with wide eyes, and whisper, "Oh, we are starting HERE?" The kind of beginning that makes the drummer lean forward on his stool, the organist crack his knuckles and flex his fingers over the keys, and the ushers start fanning the air even though nobody has shouted yet. Because listen, before I tell you ANYTHING about my life, before I unpack one testimony, before I break down one principle, before I walk you through one valley or one miracle or one moment where I thought I was going to lose my mind, I have got to start the ONLY way I know how.

THANK YOU, LORD, FOR ALL YOU HAVE DONE FOR ME.

Not later. Not after the story. Not after the examples. Not after the analysis. Not after I have built up enough credibility for you to believe me. Not after I have proven myself worthy of your attention. NOW. Right here at the front door of Chapter 1. Right here, before we even take our coats off. Right here, before we sit down and get comfortable. Right here, before the tea is poured, and the lights are dimmed, and the mood is set.

(Pastor Paul leans over the podium, eyes squinting.) "Hold on... HOLD ON... I feel something!"

Because if I do not start with gratitude, nothing else I say will make sense. If I do not begin with praise, the rest of this book will feel like a lecture instead of a testimony. If I do not start by acknowledging the God who kept me, then you will think this story is about me when it is really about HIM.

THIS CHAPTER RIGHT HERE? THIS IS THE SOUND CHECK BEFORE THE PRAISE BREAK

Have you ever been in church when the soundman is doing his testing? You know what I am talking about. The service has not started yet. People are still walking in, finding their seats, greeting each other, adjusting their hats, and checking their phones one last time before they put them on silent. And the soundman walks up to the microphone and says, "Mic check, one, two, one, two." Just a routine technical moment. Nothing spiritual about it. Just making sure the equipment works.

But then something happens. Somebody in the congregation hears that microphone click on and feels the Holy Ghost stir. And before you know it, the mic check turns into a worship service. The soundman is still adjusting levels, but the saints are already on their feet. The drummer hasn't even sat down yet, but someone is already clapping. The choir has not even walked in, but the atmosphere has already shifted. The mic check became a moment.

That is THIS. That is Chapter 1. This is the mic check that already turned into a moment. The warm-up that already caught fire. The introduction that already broke chains before we even got to the message. Because Chapter 1 is not giving you "Let me ease you in." No. We are not easing anything. Chapter 1 is giving you "Put your seatbelt on, because the glory is already creeping up the aisle." Chapter 1 is giving you "We are not waiting until Chapter 7 to shout." Chapter 1 is giving you "The ushers better stretch because somebody is about to run."

(Pastor Paul grabs the mic like it owes him money.)

I need you to understand something. This book you are holding in your hands right now did not come from a cute, peaceful, yoga-mat kind of place. I did not write this from a cabin in the woods, sipping herbal tea and wrapped in a cozy blanket. I did not write this during a quiet retreat where everything was calm, centered, and Zen. No. I wrote this from SURVIVAL. I wrote this from the trenches. I wrote this from the valley. I wrote this from a hospital bed. I wrote this at midnight, when I could not sleep because my mind would not stop racing. I wrote this from the moments when I thought I was going to lose everything.

I started this book with "God, I should have lost my mind." I started it from "God, I should have died." I started it from "God, I should have given up." I started it from "God, I should have quit." I started it from "God, I should have been another tragedy on the news, another statistic, another name people shake their heads about and say, 'That is so sad.'"

But Grace said, "Not this one." Mercy said, "I have got him." Favor said, "Cover him." Angels said, "Surround him." And God said, "LIVE."

Come on, somebody! I feel the Holy Ghost up in here!

(The organist whispers, "I know this tone... He's about to go up.")

That is why this book begins with a shout, not a whisper. A declaration, not a question. A praise, not a theory. Before I tell you anything about who I am, you need to understand WHY I am still here. You need to understand that my survival was not an accident. My healing was not luck. My breakthrough was not a coincidence. My deliverance was not random. THE LORD KEPT ME.

And if He kept me, He can keep you too. Let me say that again for somebody in the back row. If He kept me through what I went through, He can keep you through what you are going through. If He brought me out of what should have destroyed me, He can bring you out too. If He restored my mind when I thought I was losing it, He can restore yours, too. If He gave me another chance when I did not deserve it, He can give you another chance too.

So, this chapter has one assignment. One job. One purpose. One mission. To set the tone. To set the atmosphere. To bring the oil. To break the ice. To break the chains. To introduce you not to the story, but to the GOD of the story.

THIS IS NOT A NORMAL OPENING—THIS IS A DELIVERANCE SESSION IN DISGUISE

(Pastor Paul lifts one leg like the spirit hit his knee.)

You think you are reading a first chapter. You think you just opened a book to see what it is about. You think you are casually browsing, deciding whether to invest your time in these pages. But let me tell you what really happened. You really walked into a spiritual trap, and the Holy Ghost has been waiting on you. This chapter came to take some of the weight off your shoulders. This chapter came to pry fear off your chest. This chapter came to break the guilt you have been carrying for years. This chapter came to silence the lies people told you about yourself. This chapter cracked open your heart. This chapter came to wake up your praise.

Because to understand this book, understand THIS. My thank you is not polite. It is personal. My thank you is not cute. It is crucial. My thank you is not churchy. It is survival. My thank-yous are not a habit. It is healing. My thank you is not traditional. It is testimony.

When I say "Thank You, Lord," I am not saying it because it is the right thing to say. I am not saying it because it sounds good. I am not saying it because I am trying to be spiritual, religious, or holy. I am saying it because I OWE Him. I am saying it because I know what He saved me from. I am saying it because I remember where I was. I am saying it because I have not forgotten what it felt like to be broken, scared, confused, hurt, angry, lost, and desperate.

I remember the nights I cried myself to sleep. I remember the mornings I woke up and did not want to get out of bed. I remember the moments I looked in the mirror and did not recognize myself. I remember the seasons when I felt like I was drowning and nobody could hear me screaming for help. I remember the days when I smiled in public but fell apart in private. I remember the times when I preached to others about faith while my own was hanging by a thread.

And through it all, God kept me. He did not let me go. He did not give up on me. He did not walk away. He did not say, "You know what, Paul, you are too much trouble. You are too broken. You are too damaged. You are too complicated. I am done with you." No. He said, "I am not finished with you yet. I have got plans for you. I have a purpose for you. I have got a testimony coming out of this. I have got a book coming out of this. I have got a ministry coming out of this. I have got a message coming out of this. So hold on. Stay alive. Keep breathing. Keep fighting. Keep believing. Because I am about to do something in your life that is going to blow your mind."

(The reader leans forward without realizing it.)

PUT A PIN IN IT RIGHT HERE

Your survival is not an accident. Your healing is not luck. Your breakthrough is not a coincidence. God kept you on purpose, and your thank you is the receipt that proves He did not waste His time.

LET ME SET THE SCENE LIKE A PREACHER ABOUT TO OPEN HIS TEXT

Chapter 1 opens with the preacher stepping up to the pulpit, looking at the congregation with fire in his eyes, adjusting the microphone, clearing his throat, wiping his forehead with a handkerchief, and saying, "Before I preach, can we thank the Lord for a moment?" And the whole church erupts. Somebody shouts. Somebody runs. Somebody cries. Somebody lifts their hands. Somebody falls to their knees. Because they know what is about to happen. They know this is not going to be a regular service. They know the anointing is already in the building.

THAT is Chapter 1. This is not the appetizer. This is the moment the chef walks out of the kitchen and says, "Taste this real quick before we even get started." This is not the lobby. This is the sanctuary with the doors wide open and the Holy Ghost already moving. This is not the introduction. This is the ignition switch. The spark. The fuse. The starter pistol. The opening chord of the organ lets you know something powerful is about to happen.

This is the moment the saints look around at each other and say, "Oh, it is about to be one of THOSE services." You know the kind I am talking about. The kind where people leave differently from the way they came. The kind where chains break. The kind where burdens lift. The kind where healing happens. The kind where deliverance manifests. The kind where people get set free.

LET ME TELL YOU WHY CHAPTER ONE STARTS WITH THANK YOU

Because gratitude is not something I say. It is something I OWE. I owe Him for every breath I take. I owe Him for every morning I wake up, and my mind is still intact. I owe Him for every time He did not let depression swallow me whole. I owe Him for every miracle that did not look like a miracle at first. I owe Him for every door that opened when I thought I was stuck forever. I owe Him for every door He slammed shut that would have destroyed me if I had walked through it. I owe Him for not letting me become what I was fighting. I owe Him for protecting me from myself. I owe Him for covering me when I was too broken to pray. I owe Him for sending people into my life at the exact right moment. I owe Him for whispering to me in the middle of the night when I felt alone. I owe Him for keeping my heart beating when my spirit wanted to give up.

That is why Chapter 1 starts loud. That is why Chapter 1 does not tiptoe. That is why Chapter 1 does not apologize for being bold. Because God earned this praise. He earned this worship.

He earned this gratitude. He earned this testimony. He earned this book.

(The organ hums again.)

And let me tell you something else. If you're reading this and have survived something that should have killed you, you owe Him too. If you are reading these words right now and you survived something that others did not, you owe Him, too. If you are reading these words right now and you are still standing when you should be six feet under, you owe Him too. If you are reading this right now and your mind is still whole when it should be shattered, you owe Him too.

So before we go any further, before we dive into the deep stuff, before we unpack the trauma and the testimony and the trials and the triumphs, please do something with me. I need you to stop right here. I need you to put your hand on your chest. I need you to feel that heartbeat. That rhythm. That miracle. That proof that you are still here. And I need you to say it out loud, even if you are reading this in a quiet room by yourself. Say it. Mean it. Feel it.

THANK YOU, LORD, FOR ALL YOU HAVE DONE FOR ME.

BEFORE THE STORY BEGINS, THE PRAISE BEGINS

Watch this. Before I give you the WHAT, I am giving you the WHY. Before the testimony, thank you. Before the breakdown, the breakthrough. Before the journey, the shout. Before the healing, the hallelujah. Because this is not just a book. This is a celebration. This is a declaration. This is a tribute to the God who kept me when I did not deserve to be kept. This is a love letter to the One who saw me at my worst and still said, "I am not giving up on you."

And if you stick with me through this book, if you read every chapter, if you let these words sink into your spirit, if you allow the Holy Ghost to do surgery on your soul through these pages, I promise you something. By the time you get to the end, your own "THANK YOU" is going to get louder too. Your own praise will get stronger. Your own worship is going to get deeper. Your own gratitude will grow richer. Because you will remember what God brought you through. You will remember what He saved you from. You are going to remember what He delivered you out of. You are going to remember what He healed you from. You will remember what He restored in you.

And when you remember, you cannot stay quiet. When you remember, you cannot stay seated. When you remember, you cannot stay calm. When you remember, you have got to open your mouth and give Him the glory He deserves.

Come on, somebody! Ask your neighbor, "Do you remember what God did for you?"

(The organ blasts into a key change nobody was ready for.)

THIS IS JUST THE OPENING, AND WE ARE ALREADY IN A PRAISE BREAK

So let me end Chapter 1 the way it deserves to end. With the same energy we came in with. With the same fire. With the same passion. With the same boldness. With the same gratitude. With the same praise.

I want you to take a deep breath right now. I want you to close your eyes for a second. I want you to think about everything you have survived. I want you to think about every storm you have weathered. I want you to think about every battle you have fought. I want you to think about every tear you have cried. Please think about every night you did not think you would make it through. I want you to think about every morning you woke up and realized you were still here.

Now open your eyes. Look around. You are still here. You are still breathing. You are still standing. You are still fighting. You are still believing. You are still hoping. You are still trusting. You are still alive.

That is not luck. That is not a coincidence. That is not random. That is GOD.

So say it with me one more time, and this time say it like you mean it. Say it as if you have been through something. Say it like you know what it feels like to almost lose everything. Say it like you understand the weight of what I am saying. Say it like you are grateful to be alive.

THANK YOU, LORD, FOR ALL YOU HAVE DONE FOR ME!

Welcome to the book. Buckle up. Get ready. Hold on tight. Because it only gets louder from here. It only gets deeper from here. It only gets more real from here. It only gets more powerful from here.

And before we move on to Chapter 2, let me leave you with this.

(Pastor Paul lifts one leg like the spirit hit his knee.)
I SAID I'M 'BOUT TO WHOOOOOOOOOOOP IN HERE!

Somebody shout right now because you are still here! Somebody lift your hands right now because you made it through! Somebody give God praise right now because He did not let you go! The enemy thought he had you, but God said, "NOT TO-DAY!" The devil thought he could take you out, but God said,

"TOUCH NOT MY ANOINTED!" Hell thought it could destroy you, but Heaven said, "I HAVE GOT PLANS FOR THIS ONE!"

You should have lost your mind, but God kept it! You should have lost your life, but God spared it! You should have lost your faith, but God sustained it! You should have lost your hope, but God renewed it! You should have lost your joy, but God restored it!

And now you are standing on the other side of what tried to kill you, and your testimony is louder than your trauma! Your praise is stronger than your pain! Your worship is bigger than your wounds! Your gratitude is greater than your grief!

So lift your voice and let the world know: GOD IS GOOD, AND HIS MERCY ENDURES FOREVER! And if He brought you this far, He is not going to leave you now! If He kept you through that, He is going to keep you through this! If He delivered you then, He is going to deliver you again!

THANK YOU, LORD! THANK YOU, LORD! THANK YOU, LORD!

Now turn the page. Chapter 2 is waiting. And trust me, it is about to get even better.

Chapter 2

My Praise Don't Play – It Got Receipts

This Testa-Money Hit Different

SCRIPTURE

1 Chronicles 16:8-9 (KJV): "Give thanks unto the LORD, call upon his name, make known his deeds among the people. Sing unto him, sing psalms unto him, talk ye of all his wondrous works."

1 Chronicles 16:8-9 (PASTOR PAUL'S Translation): "Listen here, you better open your mouth and tell somebody what God did for you. Please do not keep it to yourself. Do not act as if you made it on your own. Do not pretend that you got here by accident. Call His name out loud. Tell the world what He did. Sing about it. Talk about it. Testify about it. Because His works are not regular, they are wondrous, and if He did something wondrous in your life, you owe Him a public praise."

(The organ hums like a lion clearing its throat.)

Listen. If Chapter 1 was the mic check, Chapter 2 is the moment when the preacher hollers, "TESTIMONY SERVICE IS NOW OPEN!" And you know EXACTLY what that means. Somebody in the back is already crying. Somebody on the left side is already rocking back and forth. One of the church mothers is digging through her purse for Kleenex. And that ONE deacon in the corner is whispering under his breath, "Don't start nothing," even though we ALL know it is TOO LATE. The Holy Ghost is already in the building. The atmosphere has already shifted. The anointing is already moving. And somebody is about to stand up and tell the truth about what God brought them through.

Because this chapter right here? This is not polite. This is not soft. This is not calm. This is not the sanitized, edited, church-approved version of my story. This is a FULL-THROT-TLE, HOLY-GHOST-FILLED, TRUTH-TELLING TESTI-MONY SESSION. And the star witness? MY LIFE. My story. My scars. My survival. My receipts. My proof that God is real and His mercy is not a theory.

(Pastor Paul pulls the glasses off his face like revelation just slapped him.)

Let me tell you something before we go any further. This chapter is not here to entertain you. This chapter is not here to impress you. This chapter is not here to make you comfortable. This chapter is here to show you WHY my gratitude is so loud. Why is my praise so intense? Why is my worship so passionate? Why is my thank you not casual? You cannot understand my thank-you until you understand my story. You cannot understand my praise until you understand my pain. You cannot understand my worship until you understand my wounds. You cannot understand my gratitude until you understand what it cost me to get here.

THIS IS NOT JUST TESTIMONY—THIS IS TESTA-MONEY

See, a testimony is when you tell what happened. You stand up in church, you clear your throat, you say, "I want to thank the Lord for what He did for me," and you tell the story. That is a testimony. But a TESTA-MONEY? That is when you tell what happened AND what it cost you. That is when you break down the price tag. That is when you show the receipts. That is when you pull out the invoices and say, "Let me show you what I paid to be standing here today."

Every tear I cried was a price. Every valley I walked through was a fee. Every storm I survived was a charge. Every battle I fought was a bill. Every night I made it through was a down payment. Every time God rescued me was an investment. And now? My gratitude is my return on God's deposit. My praise is my interest payment. My worship is my dividend. My thank you is my profit statement.

This chapter is me standing up in front of the whole room, pulling out my spiritual bank statement, and saying, **"Oh, I PAID for this praise. I EARNED this gratitude. I WORKED for this worship."**

Because before you judge my shout, you need to see the charges that hit my account.

When my body was failing and fear was sitting on my chest like a weight I could not lift, the place I once called refuge became the place where the arrows flew the hardest. The church I had bled for, prayed for, built up, and believed in—turned into a silent courtroom where the verdict had already been written... and I was not even there to defend myself.

While I was hooked up to machines, trying to hold onto life, the leaders I trusted were holding secret meetings about how to remove me. And when the hospital finally released me, thinking I was going home to love and support, I walked into a cold world where every door that once opened for me was suddenly locked.

My role? Gone.

My income? Gone.

My health insurance—during a health battle? **Gone.**

My dignity? They tried to take that too.

And let me tell you... that kind of heartbreak does not show up on a medical chart, but it will bruise your soul.

So when I say I praise loud, I praise grateful, I praise like a man who lived through something—hear me clearly:

This praise is not cheap.

It was bought with betrayal, loneliness, fear, and nights I did not think I would see morning.

It was forged in the dark.

It was birthed in pain.

I do not shout because I earned God's grace.

I shout because **grace found me when everything else walked away.**

I shout because **I lived through what was sent to bury me.**

I shout because **I am still here — and that alone is a miracle with a pulse.**

"Wait... WAIT... don't you move!"

Come on, somebody! I know I am telling the truth!

YOU CANNOT UNDERSTAND MY THANK YOU UNTIL YOU UNDERSTAND MY STORY

Let me talk plain for a minute. People see the smile, but they do not see the struggle. They see the strength, but they do not see the shaking. They see the faith, but they do not see the fear. They see the praise, but they do not see the pain. They see me standing on the platform preaching, but they do not see me on my knees in the back room praying. They see me lifting my hands in worship, but they do not see me wiping my tears in the car on the way home. They see the victory, but they do not see the valley.

But THIS chapter is not the cute version. This chapter is not the Instagram version. This chapter is not the highlight reel. This chapter is the behind-the-scenes. The unfiltered. The raw. The unedited. The part I used to hide. The version of me I did not even like looking at. The nights I did not think I would make it. The seasons where only God held me together. The moments when I wanted to quit, but something inside me said, "Not yet. Hold on. Keep going. You are closer than you think."

THIS is the chapter where I pull all that forward and say, "This is WHY I am grateful." Because gratitude does not grow in luxury. Gratitude does not grow in comfort. Gratitude does not grow in ease. Gratitude grows in SURVIVAL. Gratitude grows in the trenches. Gratitude grows in the fire. Gratitude grows in the valley. Gratitude grows in the storm. Gratitude grows in the places where you have no choice but to trust God because you have run out of every other option.

(The reader freezes.)

MY STORY IS NOT PRETTY, BUT IT IS MINE—AND GOD KEPT ME THROUGH EVERY CHAPTER

Let me say this slow enough for your soul to catch it. If you only knew the HALF of what God delivered me from, you would be shouting WITH me, not AT me. You would be praising WITH me, not judging me. You would be worshiping WITH me, not questioning me. Because my story includes the dark places. The low places. The broken places. The grieving places. The "Lord, why me?" places. The "I cannot take this anymore" places. The "I am trying to hold it together" places. The "I almost gave up" places. The "I did give up, but God picked me back up" places.

And if you have ever been THERE, not the churchy version but the REAL version, you understand why I walk heavy with this praise. You know why my worship is not casual. You understand why my gratitude is not optional. You understand why my thank you is not polite. Because I know what it feels like to be at the end of yourself. I know what it feels like to have nothing left. I know what it feels like to be so broken that you do not even know how to pray anymore. I know what it feels like to be so tired that you do not even want to fight anymore. I know what it feels like to be so hurt that you do not even want to hope anymore.

But God. Those two words. But God. He did not let me stay there. He did not let me die there. He did not let me quit there. He did not let me give up there. He reached down into the pit I was in and pulled me out. He breathed life back into my lungs. He put strength back into my legs. He put hope back into my heart. He put praise back into my mouth.

My story built my shout. My pain built my praise. My losses built my gratitude. My storms built my strength. My survival built my thank you.

(Pastor Paul walks in slow circles like he's stirring up the atmosphere.)

WHY I AM SO THANKFUL—BECAUSE GOD DID NOT LET MY STORY END WHERE IT COULD HAVE

You want to know why I praise loudly? You want to know why I work hard? You want to know why I thank God with my whole chest? Because I know EXACTLY how many ways I could have died. Not just physically, but spiritually. Emotionally. Mentally. Relationally. Financially. Purpose-wise. Destiny-wise. I could

have died in my depression. I could have died in my disappointment. I could have died in my discouragement. I could have died
in my doubt. I could have died in my despair.

But EVERY TIME something tried to bury me, God said, "Not
this one." Not today. Not this storm. Not this trap. Not this pit.
Not this attack. Not this breakdown. Not this setback. Not this
loss. Not this grief. Not this pain. Every time the enemy thought
he had me, God showed up and said, "I am not done with this
one yet. I have got plans for this one. I have a purpose for this
one. I have got a testimony coming out of this one. So back up,
devil. This one belongs to Me."

I am thankful because God interrupted what was meant to
kill me. He intercepted what was meant to destroy me. He
intervened in what was meant to end me. He interfered with
what was meant to finish me. And now I am standing here,
still breathing, still believing, still praising, still worshiping, still
thanking Him, because I should not be here, but I am.

Come on, somebody! Let me say that again for somebody in the
back row. I SHOULD NOT BE HERE, BUT I AM. And if that
does not make you want to shout, check your pulse because you
might be dead.

"The Lord is stirring something right now!"

PUT A PIN IN IT RIGHT HERE

Your gratitude is not about what you have. Your gratitude is about what you survived. Your praise is not about where you are. Your praise is about where you came from. Your thank you is not about your blessings. Your thank you is about your battles. And if God brought you through something that should have destroyed you, you owe Him more than a casual "thank you." You owe Him a TESTA-MONEY.

I AM THANKFUL BECAUSE I AM LIVING IN CHAPTERS I NEVER EXPECTED TO SEE

There were seasons I thought, "This is it. This is the end. This is the part where I disappear. This is where my story ends. This is the part where everything falls apart and never comes back together." I thought I had reached the final chapter. I thought the book was closing. I thought the credits were rolling. I thought the lights were going out. I thought it was over.

But God kept turning pages. He kept writing. He kept redirecting. He kept healing. He kept lifting. He kept restoring. He kept rebuilding. He kept renewing. He kept His hand on me even when I could not feel it. He kept speaking to me even when I could not hear it. He kept guiding me even when I could not see it. He kept protecting me even when I did not know I needed it.

And now? I am standing in chapters I only dreamed of reading. I am living in seasons I only hoped for. I am experiencing blessings I only prayed for. I am walking with the purpose I only imagined. I am fulfilling the destiny I only believed in. I am seeing miracles I only trusted for.

THIS is why I am thankful. Because God did not just SAVE me. He developed me. He did not just PRESERVE me. He prepared me. He did not just SPARE me. He upgraded me. He did not just RESCUE me. He repositioned me. He did not just DELIVER me. He promoted me. He did not just HEAL me. He elevated me.

My whole life is a receipt with the line printed on the bottom: "PAID FOR BY GRACE." Every blessing I have, Grace paid for it. Every door that opened, Grace paid for it. Every opportunity I received, Grace paid for it. Every relationship I have, Grace paid for it. Every breath I take, Grace paid for it. Every morning I wake up; Grace paid for it.

(The organ hums again.)

THIS CHAPTER IS A PRAISE BREAK DISGUISED AS A STORY

Let me tell you something else. This chapter is not just information. This chapter is a transformation. This chapter is not just words on a page. This chapter is powerful in your spirit. This chapter is not just my story. This chapter is your story too. Because if you have survived anything, and I mean ANYTHING, then you have a TESTA-MONEY too.

Maybe you survived abuse. Maybe you survived addiction. Maybe you survived betrayal. Maybe you survived bankruptcy. Maybe you survived depression. Maybe you survived a divorce. Maybe you survived the disease. Maybe you survived death. Maybe you survived disappointment. Maybe you survived a disaster. Whatever you survived, God kept you through it. And that means you have receipts too. You have proof, too. You have evidence, too. You have a testimony too. You have a TESTA-MONEY too.

And if nobody has ever told you this, let me be the first. Your survival is not an accident. Your healing is not luck. Your breakthrough is not a coincidence. Your deliverance is not random. God kept you on purpose. He saved you on purpose. He delivered you on purpose. He healed you on purpose. He restored you on purpose. And now you owe Him praise that matches what He brought you through.

Do not give God a casual thank you for a miraculous deliverance. Do not give God a quiet praise for a loud victory. Do not give God a whisper when He deserves a shout. Do not give God a nod when He deserves a dance. Do not give God a smile when He deserves a celebration.

(The organ explodes into full praise mode.)

LET ME CLOSE THIS CHAPTER THE WAY IT DESERVES

Hand to chest. Eyes lifted. Spirit ready. Heart exploding. If you have survived ANYTHING—anything significant, anything small, anything secret, anything loud, anything people know about, or anything ONLY GOD KNOWS—then say this with me right now. Say it out loud. Say it with your whole chest. Say it like you mean it. Say it as if you have been through something. Say it like you know what it cost you to be here.

THANK YOU, LORD. THIS PRAISE IS PERSONAL.

Because Chapter 2 is not a story. It is a declaration. It is a testimony. It is a survival report. It is an emotional autopsy. It is a spiritual receipt. It is a full-throated shout from somebody who KNOWS they should not be here, but God said otherwise.

This is not Chapter 2. This is my TESTA-MONEY. This is my proof. This is my evidence. This is my documentation. This is my verification. This is my confirmation. This is my validation. This is my certification that God is real, that His mercy is real, that His Grace is real, that His power is real, that His love is real, and that His faithfulness is real.

And if you are still reading this, if you made it this far, if you are still with me, then I want you to know something. Your TESTA-MONEY is just as valid as mine. Your story is just as important as mine. Your survival is just as significant as mine. Your praise is just as powerful as mine. Your gratitude is just as genuine as mine.

So please do not hold it in. Please do not keep it quiet. Do not hide it. Do not minimize it. Do not downplay it. Do not apologize for it. Let it out. Let it rise. Let it flow. Let it overflow. Let it explode.

(The organ climbs up a half-step.)

OOOOOOOOOOH I'M GETTING READY TO WHOOOOOP RIGHT NOW!

(The organist yells, "GO 'HEAD PASTOR!" as they hit the drive.)

Somebody shout right now because you have got receipts! Somebody lift your hands right now because you have got proof! Somebody give God praise right now because you have got evidence! You are not making this up! You are not exaggerating! You are not being dramatic! You really went through something, and God really brought you out!

The enemy tried to take you out, but God said, "NOT THIS ONE!" Hell tried to destroy you, but Heaven said, "I HAVE GOT PLANS FOR THIS ONE!" The devil tried to silence you, but the Holy Ghost said, "THIS ONE IS GOING TO TESTIFY!" Death tried to claim you, but Life said, "THIS ONE BELONGS TO ME!"

And now you are standing on the other side of what tried to kill you, and your TESTA-MONEY is louder than your trauma! Your praise is stronger than your pain! Your worship is bigger than your wounds! Your gratitude is greater than your grief! Your testimony is more powerful than your test!

So open your mouth and let the world know: GOD KEPT ME! GOD SAVED ME! GOD DELIVERED ME! GOD HEALED ME! GOD RESTORED ME! GOD REDEEMED ME! GOD REBUILT ME! GOD RENEWED ME! GOD REVIVED ME!

And if He did it for me, He can do it for you! If He brought me through, He can bring you through! If He kept me, He can keep you! If He saved me, He can save you! If He delivered me, He can deliver you!

THANK YOU, LORD! THANK YOU, LORD! THANK YOU, LORD!

This is not just testimony. This is TESTA-MONEY. And the receipts do not lie.

Welcome deeper into the journey. Chapter 3 is waiting. And trust me, it is about to get even more real.

Chapter 3

The Enemy Tried to Bury Me, but God Blocked the Plot

They Dug A Grave; God Built A Platform

SCRIPTURE

Psalm 91:7 (KJV): "A thousand shall fall at thy side, and ten thousand at thy right hand; but it shall not come nigh thee."

Psalm 91:7 (PASTOR PAUL'S Translation): "Chaos might be falling all around you like rain, but God looked at you and said, 'Not this one. Not today. Not like this. Not ever. I am keeping you right where you are, and nothing is going to touch you without My permission.' That is not a suggestion. That is a divine decree with your name on it."

(The organ begins a soft, suspiciously holy tremble.)

Let me tell you right now, this is not a soft chapter. This is not a gentle introduction. This is not "let us ease in and see how you feel." No, sir. No, ma'am. We are coming in HOT. We are coming in LOUD. We are coming in like somebody just yelled from the back of the sanctuary, "TESTIFY IF YOU KNOW GOD KEPT YOU!" And every soul in the building stood up at the same time because everybody has a story.

Because Chapter 3 is not a story. Chapter 3 is a survival announcement. This is the chapter where your soul stands up, takes the microphone, clears its throat, and says with its whole chest, "Tragedies are everywhere. Death is everywhere. Pain is everywhere. Loss is everywhere. But guess what? I AM STILL HERE."

Not barely here. Not limping here. Not dragging here. Not crawling here. Not hanging on by a thread here. HERE. Fully here. Alive here. Breathing here. Present here. Purposeful here. Protected here. Preserved here. And I do not care who likes it or who expected you not to make it or who wrote you off or who counted you out or who planned your funeral in their mind. You are STILL HERE.

(Pastor Paul stops mid-sentence like heaven tapped him on the shoulder.)

THIS CHAPTER COMES IN LIKE A FIRE ALARM—NO WARNING, ALL SMOKE

This one does not walk in politely. It kicks the door open like, "I have got something to say, and you are going to listen." Because when you have lived long enough, been hit enough, lost enough, cried enough, fought enough, fallen apart enough, you do not start quietly. You start with a WAR CRY. And this chapter starts with the kind of energy that makes the organist look up like, "Oh, we are starting HERE today?"

Because listen. When you have seen tragedy up close, not on the news, not in the headlines, not in somebody else's life, but in YOUR house, YOUR body, YOUR bank account, YOUR mind, YOUR childhood, YOUR relationships, YOUR family, YOUR marriage, YOUR career, YOUR health, and YOUR faith, and yet somehow, someway, against all logic, against all odds, against all predictions, against all statistics, YOU ARE STILL HERE, you do not whisper after that. You holler.

You do not tiptoe into gratitude. You run into it. You do not ease into praise. You explode into it. You do not casually mention your survival. You declare it. You announce it. You testify about it. You shout about it. You let the whole world know that you should not be here, but God said otherwise.

"Hold my mule... HOLD MY MULE!"

THIS CHAPTER OPENS WITH A TESTIMONY DIS-GUISED AS A DECLARATION

Truth is, I did not plan to write this chapter like this. It wrote to me. Because there comes a moment in every survivor's life where you look around and realize, "I should have been gone. I should have been broken. I should have been addicted. I should have been lost. I should have been stuck. I should have been grieving forever. I should have been OUTTA here."

But somehow, somehow, SOMEHOW, you woke up anyway. You inhaled anyway. You got dressed anyway. You kept moving anyway. You kept living anyway. You are reading this book anyway. That is not random. That is not luck. That is not a coincidence. That is not good fortune. That is not positive thinking. That is GOD WITH A CAPITAL G, interrupting tragedy with mercy and replacing what should have killed you with what healed you.

Let me tell you where I was when this chapter started writing itself. I was sitting in my bedroom, the one where the carpet knows all my tears by name, and the room was quiet in that spooky "God is about to say something" way. I was not praying. I was not journaling. I was not even trying to be deep. I was breathing. Barely. Because this was around the time cancer tried to punk me. This was around the time fear kept climbing into bed with me like it paid rent. This was around the time the doctors' voices got really serious and really soft at the same time, and THAT is when you know you are in trouble.

This was one of those nights when you do not need a sermon. You ARE the sermon. And out of nowhere, the same God who kept me in that radiation room, the same God who walked me through grief when Mama and Daddy went home, the same God who did not let me die from the stress I swallowed for years, THAT God leaned in and whispered, "You are STILL here."

And when He said it, OH, something MOVED in me. The air shifted. My chest expanded. My soul stood up like, "Is this roll call for survivors? Because I am present."

(The reader clutches their invisible pearls.)

Come on, somebody! I feel the Holy Ghost up in here!

THIS IS NOT A REGULAR CHAPTER—THIS IS A SURVIVOR'S ROLL CALL

Have you ever been in one of those church services where the preacher says, "If God kept you from ANYTHING, just wave your hand!" And EVERYBODY waves? Even the quiet people? Even the folks who only came because their grandma made them? Even the ones who usually sit in the back with their arms folded? That is this chapter.

This chapter is the part of the service where everybody stands up because EVERYBODY survived something. And this chapter opens with one truth. If tragedy is commonplace, then the fact that you are still alive is a MIRACLE. A miracle with your name on it. A miracle that has receipts. A miracle that has evidence. A miracle that has chapters behind it. A miracle that has witnesses. A miracle that has documentation. A miracle that has proof.

You are not here by default. You are here by DESIGN. You are not here by accident. You are here by ASSIGNMENT. You are not here by chance. You are here by CHOICE. God's choice. Heaven's choice. The choice that said, "This one stays. This one lives. This one survives. This one overcomes. This one testifies. This one matters."

THE CHAPTER 3 VIBE—"I SHOULD NOT BE HERE, BUT I AM."

This is the chapter where I walk up to the pulpit of your heart, lean on it, look you right in the eyes, and say, "Listen. You KNOW good and well you should not be here." And you know it is true because something in you says, "Yeah. You are right. I should not be here."

This chapter starts like a praise break because it IS one. This chapter starts loud because the miracle was loud. This chapter starts bold because tragedy was bold. This chapter starts with fire because survival is fire. This chapter starts with YOU because YOU are the evidence. Evidence that mercy works. Evidence that grace covers. Evidence that protection is real. Evidence that God blocks things you never even knew were coming.

Yes, sir. Yes, ma'am. This one is PERSONAL.

(Pastor Paul throws his head back like he just saw the miracle.)

THE ROOM WAS DARK, BUT I WOKE UP ANYWAY

Let me step into this chapter like I am stepping onto a pulpit, with my shoes already off, because this is holy ground. This chapter is not casual. This chapter is not soft. This right here? This is the chapter where the hairs on your arm stand up because your SPIRIT recognizes itself.

See, people do not talk enough about those quiet resurrections. The moments when nobody laid hands on you. Nobody prayed you through. Nobody knew what you were carrying. But God touched you in the dark, and your spirit said, "Let there be light."

Let me tell you something real. Before I ever testified with a microphone, before I ever wrote a book with my name in bold letters, before I ever became "Pastor Paul" to people around the world, I was just a man sitting in a dim room trying to remember why living mattered. And God told me, "Because you are not done yet."

Say what you want, but nothing will rearrange your soul like hearing Heaven tell you that death had a plan, but it failed.

PUT A PIN IN IT RIGHT HERE

Your survival is not a coincidence. Your healing is not luck. Your deliverance is not random. God kept you through what should have killed you because He has plans for you that are bigger than your pain, stronger than your struggle, and more powerful than your past.

THE MOMENT WHERE YOU REALIZE GOD SAVED YOU FROM WHAT YOU DID NOT EVEN SEE

Have you ever had a moment so heavy your whole soul hits the brakes? That was me. Sitting in that dark room, trying to figure out how I STILL had breath in my body after everything I have lived through. Because let us be honest. I did not survive because I am tough. I did not survive because I am smart. I did not survive because I am "anointed." I survived because God stepped between me and something that had ALREADY claimed me.

And that is when the revelation hit me like a bus. The danger I saw was not the danger that almost killed me. The REAL danger was the stuff I never even knew was coming. You'd better hear me today. Some tragedies you OUTRAN, but some tragedies

GOD CANCELLED before they even got your address. And THAT is why your thank you hits different.

(The organ shifts into that sanctified buzz.)

THE WORLD WAS BURNING, AND SOMEHOW YOU STILL HAD BREATH

Turn on the news. Scroll social media. Listen to people's stories. Tragedy is not a surprise anymore. It is the whole atmosphere. People are dying too young. Diseases showing up uninvited. Accidents happening out of nowhere. Violence is increasing. Worry rising. Fear spreading like smoke. Everywhere you look, somebody is losing, somebody is hurting, and somebody is going under.

But YOU? YOU woke up. YOU got another day. YOU got another breath. YOU made it out of the house. YOU did not lose your mind. YOU did not collapse under the weight. You are STILL here. Please do not act like you're brand new to it. This is not a small thing. This is a miracle wearing your clothes.

THE DAY I REALIZED "THIS SHOULD HAVE BEEN ME"

Let me confess something.
There were days during my cancer journey when I would sit in that waiting room, looking into the eyes of people fighting

the same battle I was fighting—except their stories were ending while mine kept getting another chapter.

And there was one night... one night I will never forget.

The room was dim.
Machines humming low.
Hope and fear sharing the same air.

I heard a soft rustling, almost like a whisper of fabric brushing against eternity. The presence lingered near the bed beside mine — the bed of the man who had become my silent companion in that space of healing and heartbreak.

He did not move.
He did not breathe.
Time froze.

And then the truth washed over me:
He was gone.

The medical staff came in with quiet reverence, no chaos, no shouting—just that sacred hush that fills a room when a soul steps into eternity. And as they gently prepared his body, I lay there, staring at the ceiling, realizing:

It could have been me.

It *should* have been me—according to every medical report and every bleak prognosis spoken over my life.

But God... kept me.

And in that moment, a question rose up inside me like a trembling whisper:

"Why them? Why not me?"

Not from guilt.
Not from comparison.
But from raw, unfiltered gratitude.

Because tragedy does not follow rules.
It does not pick and choose based on goodness or badness.
It does not look at church attendance or prayer life.
It does not skip over the righteous.

It strikes where it wants.
It lands where it lands.

But somehow—SOMEHOW—God looked at *me* and said,

"Not this one."

I do not know why.
I do not know what He saw in me.

I do not know what made Him say "live" when everything else said "die."

But I know this:

I am still here.
And that means something.

That means I owe Him.
I owe Him my voice.
I owe Him my testimony.
I owe Him my praise.
I owe Him my worship.
I owe Him my gratitude.
I owe Him my life.

Come on, somebody!
Let me run that back for the folks in the balcony, the ushers in the aisle, and the ones holding their breath:

If you are STILL here...
you OWE Him something!

I FEEL MY HELLLLLLLLP COMING ON!

WHEN YOU REALIZE YOUR LIFE IS A "BUT GOD" STORY

Here is the moment that will make your soul shout. When you finally wake up to the fact that almost EVERYTHING in your life starts with two words. BUT GOD. I should have died, BUT GOD. I should have lost my mind, BUT GOD. I should have stayed broken, BUT GOD. I should have been crushed by grief, BUT GOD. I should have drowned in depression, BUT GOD. I should have been stuck in fear forever, BUT GOD. I should have given up on life, BUT GOD. I should have faded away quietly, BUT GOD.

Those two words? They are your entire autobiography. And let me tell you, when you start SEEING the "but God" moments, you praise differently. You walk differently. You breathe differently. You make different decisions. You start giving yourself grace. You start recognizing the favor in your life. You stop apologizing for being chosen. You stop pretending your survival was random. Because YOU KNOW, deep in your soul, that Heaven intervened.

WHEN SURVIVAL TURNS INTO RESPONSIBILITY

This part right here? This is where the shift happens. It is when you stop asking, "Why did I survive?" And start asking, "What am I supposed to DO with my survival?" Because surviving is not just a blessing. It is an ASSIGNMENT. Every breath you still have is because God entrusted you with something. Every morning you wake up is because there is someone you are sup-posed to impact. Every tear you outlived is because there is a message in your bones that somebody else needs to hear.

You did not survive cancer to stay quiet. You did not survive grief to play small. You did not survive trauma to disappear. You did not survive attacks to hold your testimony hostage. You survived because Heaven said, "Your story is someone else's key."

(The organist modulates like they got possessed by a praise break.)

WHEN YOU REALIZE YOU ARE WALKING EVIDENCE

This is the part where you stand up straight and remember who you are. You are not an accident. You are not random. You are not a lucky break. You are not a coincidence. You are EVIDENCE. Walking evidence. Breathing evidence. Talking evidence. Praising evidence. Evidence that God still saves. Evidence that God still heals. Evidence that God still restores. Evidence that God still blocks tragedy. Evidence that purpose is stronger than pain. Evidence that destiny is louder than disaster.

Your life is a billboard that reads, "I AM STILL HERE."

WHEN YOU REALIZE YOU OUTLIVED WHAT TRIED TO ERASE YOU

Let me say something really heavy. You outlived stuff that was not supposed to LET you live. You outlived trauma. You outlived heartbreak. You outlived sickness. You outlived grief. You outlived fear. You outlived disappointment. You outlived betrayal. You outlived the attacks you KNEW about and the attacks you DID NOT.

Listen. People do not even understand your praise because they do not understand your SURVIVAL. This chapter is your reminder. The grave was expecting you, but God revoked the invitation.

THE MOMENT YOU FINALLY TELL HELL, "YOU MISSED."

This part right here? This is where your spirit stands up in full armor, with your feet planted, your back straight, and your voice shaking the atmosphere. This is the moment you tell every demon, every diagnosis, every heartbreak, every lie, every storm, and every trauma, "YOU. MISSED. ME."

You did not hit your target. You did not finish your assignment. You did not take me out. You did not get the victory. You did not steal my purpose. You did not end my story. You did not erase my future. I am STILL here. And I am not whispering it. I am declaring it.

Come on, somebody! Ask your neighbor, "Did the enemy miss you, too?"

(Pastor Paul screams, "YEAH, YEAH, YEAH.)

TRAGEDIES MAY BE COMMONPLACE, BUT SO IS GOD'S PROTECTION

Let me flip your perspective real quick. Yes, tragedy is everywhere. We see it. We hear it. We feel it. But you know what ELSE is everywhere? GOD. IS. EVERYWHERE. And His protection? His mercy? His grace? His hand? His covering? His angels? His barrier? His blood? Even MORE commonplace.

Tragedy shows up, but so does GOD. Therefore, the presence of danger is not the absence of God. The presence of chaos is not stronger than the presence of Christ. You walked THROUGH the valley because God walked you OUT of it.

THE WEIGHT OF YOUR SURVIVAL IS HOLY

Your survival is not just a story. It is a SACRED THING. Your life is not ordinary. Your breath is not casual. Your testimony is not optional. Every time you inhale, Heaven is saying, "Purpose still lives here." Every time you exhale, you are participating in a miracle that your past thought had destroyed. Every sunrise you witness is God reminding you that you are STILL part of His plan.

This is why you cannot play small. This is why you cannot shrink back. This is why you cannot dim your light. This is why you cannot pretend you do not matter. BECAUSE YOU DO. You matter so much that tragedy could not keep you. Death could not claim you. Fear could not freeze you. And the enemy could not END you.

THE REAL REASON YOU ARE STILL HERE

Let us bring it all home in one sentence. You are still here because God refused to let tragedy finish what it started. You are here because purpose has work to do. You are here because your voice is needed. You are here because your story will set somebody free. You are here because your future is too important. You are here because your survival is too powerful. You are here because God said "YES" when everything else said "NO."

And I am going to say something bold. You did not just survive tragedy. You EMBARRASSED it. You walked out of storms that were expected to bury you. You shook off attacks that were expected to cripple you. You stood back up after life threw you to the ground. You walked out of the fire without smelling like smoke. You did not just survive. You overcame.

(The organ explodes into full praise mode.)

Now let me tell you why I shout like I shout! Because when I look back over my life—the cancer, the grief, the depression, the fear, the losses, the nights I cried, the days I broke, the moments I wanted to quit—when I look back and see that I am STILL HERE? Oh, my soul gets LOUD! My heart gets full! My praise gets messy! My gratitude gets wild! My spirit gets to dancing!

And I shout with everything in me: "THANK YOU, LORD! I MADE IT!" I made it through danger! I made it through loss! I made it through heartbreak! I made it through sickness! I made it through trauma! I made it through fear! I made it through EVERYTHING that tried to break me!

And now I declare: I am still here! Still breathing! Still healing! Still fighting! Still growing! Still chosen! Still covered! Still protected! Still PURPOSEFUL!

Somebody shout right now because tragedy tried to take you out, but God said, "NOT THIS ONE!" Hell tried to destroy you, but Heaven said, "I HAVE GOT PLANS FOR THIS ONE!" The devil tried to silence you, but the Holy Ghost said, "THIS ONE IS GOING TO TESTIFY!" Death tried to claim you, but Life said, "THIS ONE BELONGS TO ME!"

And if you know like I know, God kept you through things you did not tell a soul about, then lift your spirit right now and say, "THANK YOU, LORD! I AM STILL HERE!"

Because tragedies may be commonplace, but so is the mercy of God! And His mercy is stronger than any tragedy! His grace is bigger than any grief! His power is greater than any pain! His love is louder than any loss!

THANK YOU, LORD! THANK YOU, LORD! THANK YOU, LORD!

Welcome deeper into the journey. Chapter 4 is waiting. And trust me, it is about to get even more powerful.

Chapter 4

The Devil Filed My Death Notice, but God Rejected the Request

Heaven said, "Not today"

SCRIPTURE

Isaiah 59:19 (KJV): "When the enemy shall come in like a flood, the Spirit of the Lord shall lift up a standard against him."

Isaiah 59:19 (PASTOR PAUL'S Translation): "Trouble rolled up on me as it had me on its calendar, like it had my address memorized, like it had been planning this attack for months. But God stepped in front of it, put His hand up, and said, 'Nah. Not this one. Not today. Not ever. You are not touching what I am protecting.' And that is not a suggestion. That is a divine restraining order."

(The organ hums like it's thinking about running.)

Let me go ahead and warn you right now. Chapter 4 is not coming in quietly. It is not tiptoeing in like a shy visitor who came late to church and is trying not to disturb anybody. No. This chapter is bursting through the door with the energy of a Sunday morning praise break, with the usher board already sweating and the drummer doing stretches because he knows what is about to happen.

Because THIS chapter? THIS ONE is personal. This is the chapter I do not whisper. This is the chapter I do not sugarcoat. This is the chapter I do not edit for comfort. This is the chapter where I look you dead in your soul and say, I SHOULD HAVE BEEN A STATISTIC, BUT GOD BLOCKED IT.

That is not drama. That is not an exaggeration. That is not "church talk." That is a fact. That is MY life. That is MY story. That is MY testimony. And if you have ever walked through hell with the smell of smoke still clinging to you, if you have ever survived something you have not even told NOBODY about, you already know. This chapter is about to snatch wigs, edges, pride, trauma, and maybe your feelings. Good. You needed that.

(Pastor Paul snatches the towel off the pulpit like the devil just challenged him.)

THE "REAL TALK" INTRO: THIS CHAPTER COST ME SOMETHING

Before we go any further, let me say this. This is not just a chapter for me. This is a receipt. A survival receipt. A grace receipt. A "Lord, it should have been me" receipt. Somebody shouts, "I got receipts!" Because I have lived through stuff that should have put my face on a T-shirt with doves flying behind me and a choir singing softly in the background.

I am talking about REAL stuff. The danger I ignored. The warnings I dismissed. The people I trusted who nearly wrecked my life. The fear that almost had me frozen. The sickness that tried to grip me. The depression that wanted to bury me. The worry that tried to suffocate me. The cancer diagnosis that attempted to write a chapter God never signed. But through it all, God's protection kept me alive and hopeful.

YES, that part is personal. When I sat in that doctor's office, hearing a word nobody wants to hear, my spirit did not crumble. It screamed, "Lord, BLOCK IT." And guess what? He did. He brought me through the treatment. He carried me through the fear. He covered me through the pain. He held me when I could not hold myself. He kept me ALIVE to write THIS right here. That is why this chapter hits different.

"Y'all don't hear me..."

THIS IS NOT A SOFT OPENING—THIS IS ME SLAMMING THE MIC DOWN ON HELL'S HEAD

Because let us be honest. A lot of the stuff that almost took me out was not the devil. It was ME. My choices. My stubbornness. My trying-to-fix-everybody habits. My "I got it, Lord" attitude. My "I am strong enough" foolishness. My "I can handle this" pride. My "I do not need help" independence. My "I will be fine" lies.

And YET, God STILL blocked it. Blocked the disaster. Blocked the heartbreak. Blocked the wrong people. Blocked the danger. Blocked the trap. Blocked the depression. Blocked the diagnosis from becoming a death sentence. Blocked the attack that I did not even see coming. Blocked the consequences I earned. Blocked the outcomes I deserved.

And every time I look back over my life, not the polished version, not the pastor version, not the strong version, but the REAL version, I say the same thing every time. "Lord, I should have been a statistic, but You did not let that happen."

Come on, somebody! I know I am telling the truth!

CHAPTER 4 STARTS WITH TRUTH AND A TESTIMONY

So let me tell you right now. This chapter is not cute. This chapter is not sweet. This chapter is not a Hallmark card. This chapter is me, standing in front of a FULL church, testifying with my whole chest, organ humming behind me, sweat towel in my hand, saying, "You do not know what He brought me out of. You do not know what He saved me from. You do not know the nights I should have died. You do not know the traps I walked into. You do not know how close I came to losing ME."

And yet, I am still here. Breathing. Walking. Writing. Preaching. Smiling. Surviving. Thriving. HEALED. Not because I deserved it. Not because I earned it. Not because I was smart. Not because I was holy. Not because I was careful. But because God BLOCKED IT.

(Pastor Paul stomps one foot like the spirits of 50 ancestors just rose up.)

THE CHAPTER 4 PROMISE

Before you read one more word, let me give you the theme. This is the chapter where we talk about everything that should have taken you out but did not. This is the chapter where you finally admit you were saved from the consequences you earned and disasters you deserved. This is the chapter where you stop hiding how close you came to quitting, running, breaking, collapsing, walking away, or giving up.

This is the chapter where you say, with complete clarity, complete honesty, and full praise, "I am alive because God said NO when death, tragedy, and foolishness said YES."

Welcome to Chapter 4. Take a breath. Sit up. Prepare your spirit. Because this chapter right here? This is not literature. This is deliverance. This is not writing. This is worship. This is not storytelling. This is survival on display. Let us walk into it together. And by the end, you are going to holler with me, "I SHOULD HAVE BEEN A STATISTIC, BUT GOD BLOCKED IT!"

(The organ hits a menacing chord.)

THE OPENING—WHEN THE MEMORY SLAPPED ME IN THE FACE

Let me take you back. I was not praying. I was not fasting. I was not deep. I was not even thinking holy thoughts. I was sitting in my car in a parking lot, minding my business and tearing up some fries I KNOW I did not need. And out of NOWHERE, a memory slapped me. Not tapped me. Not tapped on the shoulder like, "You remember?" I mean a FULL SLAP, like it was offensive, I forgot it happened.

This is a memory I do not just recall—I *relive.* A night where I **COULD HAVE died.** A night that still walks up on me sometimes and taps me on the shoulder to remind me, "You were supposed to be gone."

I was twenty-three. Young, hopeful, and trying to figure out my place in a world that felt too big for my little fears. Then suddenly I was in this cold room filled with the sharp, sterile smell of a hospital—you know that smell that makes your spirit tense up before your body knows why.

A young doctor stepped in, eyes flat, voice steady, and she dropped words on me like bricks falling from heaven with no warning.
She said I would not live to see thirty. No compassion. No pause. No human softness. Just a sentence... as if she were reading it off a clipboard God had never signed.

"Set your house in order."
That was not advice. That was a verdict.
That was the death notice.

In that moment, I felt the room tilt. Because all it would have taken—one shift, one misdiagnosis, one divine delay not showing up on time—and I would not have been breathing long enough to tell you this story.

Have you ever frozen mid-chew? When your mouth forgets how to work but your mind takes off running laps? That was me.

Sitting in the car afterward, staring out the windshield, fries turning cold on the seat beside me like a silent witness. And all I could whisper was:

"Lord... I really should have been a statistic."

And right there—in that quiet space between fear and revelation—something rose up inside me. Not loud, not flashy, not churchy.
Just steady. Just sure.

"Then tell it."

So here I am.
Still breathing.
Still standing.
Still testifying about a death that never happened.

LET US TELL THE TRUTH—SOME OF MY TROUBLE WAS MY OWN FAULT

Oh yes. Let us not play holy. Some of the stuff that almost took me out? I VOLUNTEERED FOR IT. I walked right into danger like the devil had coupons, and I wanted the discount. I signed up for relationships with "WARNING" written on their foreheads. I signed up for friends who did not want to see me win. I signed up for rooms I had no business being in. I signed up for responsibilities that were choking me. I signed up for battles that were not my assignment. I signed up for fights that were not mine to fight. I signed up to rescue people who did not even want to be saved.

Listen. Let me be honest. Some of the tragedies in my life were not spiritual attacks. They were bad decisions. And if you are honest with yourself? You have got a few of those too. Do you ever look back at your past self and think, "Lord, WHY did You let me survive ME?"

Because THAT is the miracle. Not surviving the devil. Surviving the version of yourself who did not love you yet. Did not protect you yet. Did not value you yet. Did not know who you were yet. But watch this. Even THEN, God blocked disaster. Not because I deserved protection, but because He was not finished.

(Reader pauses to catch their breath.)

THE CONSEQUENCES I SHOULD HAVE RECEIVED, BUT DID NOT

This part right here? Whew. Listen to me clearly. If God had allowed the FULL consequences of some of my decisions, I would be dead. I would be gone. I would be forgotten. I would be "one of those sad stories." I would be a memory, with soft piano music in the background. I would be "gone too soon." I would say, "He was talented, but..." I would be a cautionary tale.

BUT I AM NOT. You know what I am? A survivor of mercy. A product of grace. Somebody whose PURPOSE outran their mistakes. God blocked outcomes even when He let me walk into the situation. Who does that? GOD. Only God.

Come on, somebody! Ask your neighbor, "Did God block something for you, too?"

WHEN THE ENEMY CAME IN LIKE A FLOOD—AND GOD LIFTED A WALL

Let me say this with fire. The devil did not come at me gently. He did not walk. He did not creep. He came in like a FLOOD. A flood is FAST. A flood is VIOLENT. A flood is UNEXPECTED. A flood is DESTRUCTIVE. A flood is TOTAL.

And some seasons of my life felt EXACTLY like that. Sickness is flooding my body. Grief floods my soul. Stress is flooding my mind. Fear floods my nights. Pressure flooding my days. Loneliness is flooding my heart. Trauma floods my memories.

But the scripture says, "The Spirit of the Lord shall LIFT UP a standard." Meaning, when the flood came, God built a wall in front of me that the flood COULD NOT CROSS.

Do you know what that looks like in real life? Cancer tried to roll in like a flood, but God built a wall. Stress wanted to drown me like a flood, but God built a wall. Fear tried to swallow me whole, but God built a wall. Depression tried to take my breath, but God built a wall. Grief tried to bury me alive, but God built a wall.

And listen, that wall was not there because I was strong. It showed up because GOD IS.

(The organ hums again.)

GOD'S "ABSOLUTELY NOT" SAVED MY LIFE

There were moments in my life when I was running straight toward disaster. Full speed. Eyes closed. Thinking, I knew what I was doing. And right before I stepped off the cliff of a terrible decision, something in me, something holy, something protective, something stern, rose up and said, "ABSOLUTELY NOT."

God's "ABSOLUTELY NOT" saved me from people who meant me harm, jobs that would have drained me, relationships that would have broken me, paths that were never mine, rooms I was not assigned to, opportunities that were really traps, storms I was not built for, and outcomes I was not ready to face.

God said, "If he walks into this, he will not recover." And He BLOCKED IT. And when God blocks a thing? It stays blocked.

PUT A PIN IN IT RIGHT HERE

The enemy aimed to take you out, but purpose would not let you die. You are not alive by accident. You are alive because your ASSIGNMENT refused to let go of you. Your survival is not luck. Your survival is divine intervention. Your survival is proof that God has plans for you that are bigger than your past.

STORY TIME—THE DAY I ALMOST MADE A DECISION I COULD NOT UNDO

Let me tell you about the moment that STILL makes my soul tremble—the moment I do not talk about lightly, the moment that feels like touching fire with my bare hands.

There was a day when I was **done**.
Not regularly done.
Not "I need a nap" done.
I mean **DONE done**—mentally, emotionally, spiritually, and physically emptied out like somebody had scooped the life out of my chest.

I was tired.
Tired of fighting battles nobody saw.
Tired of hoping for miracles that felt delayed.
Tired of believing when everything around me kept breaking.

Tired of wearing the strong mask for everybody else while I was bleeding behind it.

Tired of the pain in my body.

Tired of the grief in my heart.

Tired of holding up a world that was crushing me.

And in that exhaustion, I made a plan—a bad plan.

A dangerous plan.

A **"my future will NEVER recover from this"** plan.

I got into my car.

Turned the key.

Hands shaking so hard the steering wheel felt like it was pulsing.

I was standing at the intersection of despair and no return.

And then it happened—that dark whisper.

That cold thought.

That lie that creeps in when your soul is starving:

"Just end it. Just make the pain stop."

Suicide suddenly looked like an exit ramp—a way out of the betrayal, the loss, the sickness, and the cruelty of people I once trusted.

I had lost my business.

Lost my church.

Nearly lost my faith.

And in that suffocating, shadowed moment...
A flicker of light pierced through.

I heard the words of Rev. James Cleveland float back into my spirit like a rope thrown into deep water:

"I don't believe He brought me this far to leave me."

Something in me—something stubborn, something holy, something still breathing—sparked back to life.
I could not let *this* be the end of my story.

My heart was pounding.
My purpose felt like it was slipping right through my fingers.

And then—right before I pulled off—my radio,
WHICH WAS OFF,
turned on.

Not to music.
Not to preaching.
Not to gospel.
Not to worship.

STATIC.
LOUD static.
Like heaven slammed its fist on the table.

And right there in that moment, God spoke so clearly it rattled my bones:

"Don't you dare ruin your life today."

And I froze.
Because even in my darkest hour, even when I was ready to surrender the pen that writes my story...

God still refused to let me end the chapter.

I broke right there. Cried in the car like a child. Like grief was finally coming out of my bones. And right there in the driver's seat, I realized God BLOCKED the worst decision I was about to make. Purpose saved me. Mercy saved me. Grace saved me. God's voice saved me.

And I think about that day often, because that was the day I realized my life belonged to God in a way I had never understood before.

(Pastor Paul drags a towel across his face like he's fighting the humidity and the Holy Ghost at the same time.)

I SHOULD HAVE BEEN A STATISTIC—BUT PURPOSE SAID "NO."

Let me break this down. I should have been dead, broken, lost, hopeless, addicted, grieving forever, emotionally crushed, mentally gone, spiritually empty, financially wrecked, relationally destroyed, and PURPOSELESS.

But the purpose GOD put inside me said, "NO. I STILL need his voice. I STILL need his testimony. I STILL need his creativity. I STILL need his story. I STILL need his ministry. I STILL need his impact. He STILL has work to do."

Purpose would not let me die. Purpose would not let me quit. Purpose would not let me walk away. Purpose would not let me give up. Purpose would not let me end things early. Purpose kept whispering in my spirit, "Hold on." And here I am.

GOD BLOCKED ATTACKS YOU DID NOT EVEN KNOW ABOUT

You know what makes me shout? Not just what God saved me FROM, but what He saved me BEFORE. There are accidents you never had, people you never met, rooms you never entered, sicknesses you never caught, traps you never fell into, betrayals that never reached you, dangers that never touched you, and heartbreaks that never happened, because God blocked them BEFORE they got to your door.

Protection is not just seeing angels. It is not SEEING the disasters they blocked. You do not even KNOW the full number of miracles that make up your life.

Come on, somebody! Let me say that again for somebody in the back row. You do not even know how many times God saved you from something you never saw coming!

THE MOMENT YOU REALIZE YOUR SURVIVAL IS YOUR MINISTRY

At some point, usually in the quiet, you begin to understand. I am alive for a REASON. Not just to survive. Not just to pay bills. Not just to exist. Not just to try again tomorrow. You are alive because someone needs your wisdom, someone needs your story, someone needs your voice, someone needs your strength, someone needs your authenticity, someone needs your ministry, and someone needs your survival to inspire THEIR survival.

You did not live through all this to sit silent. Your life is a sermon God already preached through your survival. Now you have to TESTIFY.

(The organ begins to swell.)

NAWWWW I CAN'T HOLD IT... I'M ABOUT TO WHOOOOOOOP!

(The organ takes off like it's chasing glory itself.)

Let me close this chapter the only way it deserves to be closed. With a PRAISE. Because when I look back over my life—the

cancer, the grief, the nights I almost quit, the storms that nearly broke me, the attacks that came like floods, the danger I
survived, the fear I fought, the pain I carried, and the tears I
cried—and see that I am STILL HERE? My soul goes OFF!

I shout, "THANK YOU, LORD, FOR BLOCKING EVERY
TRAP!" "THANK YOU, LORD, FOR SAVING MY LIFE!"
"THANK YOU, LORD, FOR PROTECTING MY PUR-
POSE!" "THANK YOU, LORD! I SHOULD HAVE BEEN
A STATISTIC, BUT I AM STILL HERE!"

Somebody lift your hands right now because the devil had
your name on a tombstone, but God said, "RETURN TO
SENDER!" Hell tried to claim you, but Heaven said, "THIS
ONE BELONGS TO ME!" The enemy tried to write your obit-
uary, but God said, "I AM NOT DONE WITH THIS ONE
YET!"

And if you KNOW this chapter is your story too, lift your
spirit with me and say, "THANK YOU, LORD, FOR EVERY-
THING YOU DID NOT LET HAPPEN!"

You should have been gone, but you are here! You should have
been broken, but you are healed! You should have been lost,
but you are found! You should have been destroyed, but you
are restored! You should have been a statistic, but you are a
TESTIMONY!

THANK YOU, LORD! THANK YOU, LORD! THANK YOU, LORD!

Welcome deeper into the journey. Chapter 5 is waiting. And trust me, it is about to get even more powerful.

Chapter 5

God Assigned an Angel to Me Without My Permission

And He Kept Me Alive

S CRIPTURE

Psalm 121:7 (KJV): "The Lord shall preserve thee from all evil: he shall preserve thy soul."

Psalm 121:7 (PASTOR PAUL'S Translation): "God said, 'I am keeping watch over you even when you are not watching yourself. I am guarding your steps, your soul, your silly decisions, your midnight mistakes, your daytime drama, and everything in between. You think you are out here alone? No, I have been protecting you from things you will never even know tried to destroy you.'"

(The organ starts with a quiet, midnight hum.)

Let me tell you right now, this chapter is not soft. This one right here? This is the chapter where you put the book down halfway through and say out loud, "Wait, God REALLY kept me." This is the chapter where your spirit grabs a folding chair, sets it right in the middle of your heart, and says, "Come on, Pastor Paul, tell it." So let me walk you into this slowly. Because the way Chapter 5 hit ME is the way I want it to hit YOU.

I was sitting in my living room, not praying, not journaling, not fasting, not trying to be deep or spooky or mystical, just sitting. Feet up. Mind tired. Body worn out. Soul somewhere between "Lord, help" and "I do not have it today." The couch was sagging like it was tired too. The lamp was leaning, as if it needed prayer. The room was quiet in that serious "God is coming for your edges" kind of way.

I turned on the news, and chaos jumped out of the TV like it was tired of being inside. Wars everywhere. Violence everywhere. Disease everywhere. Prices are going up like they are training for Everest. People are losing their minds, their peace, their footing, and their hope. I watched it all and whispered one simple sentence. "Lord, how did I make it this far?"

(Pastor Paul leans forward, whispering like he's cracking open heaven's diary.)

And let me tell you something. Your spirit will talk back when the question is real enough. Because instantly, and I do mean

INSTANTLY, my spirit clapped back with attitude. "Because God has been protecting you like you are important."

Whew. I froze. Even the couch froze. Even the dust in the corner froze. Even the lamp stopped judging me for not fixing it. Because I heard the truth. "God has been watching over you longer than you have known how to watch over yourself."

And right there, sitting in a living room that looked like a commercial for "Real Life, Not Instagram," I felt something settle in my chest. "I SHOULD NOT BE HERE. BUT GOD PROTECTED ME EVERY. STEP. OF. THE. WAY."

YOUR ENTIRE LIFE IS A RECEIPT OF HIS PROTECTION

See, it is one thing to say God is good. It is another thing to realize your ENTIRE LIFE is a receipt of His protection. I am talking about protection through the cancer, the fear, the grief of losing Mama and Daddy, the nights the radiation room felt colder than your bones, the stress that tried to sit on your chest like a weighted blanket, the anxiety that tried to drag you out of your own head, the mistakes that should have drowned you, the people who should have broken you, the depression that tried to erase you, the childhood wounds that tried to shape you, the health scares, the close calls, the roads you should have never driven down, the places you should have never survived, and the decisions that should have ended your story.

And yet, here you are. Breathing. Healing. Laughing again. Publishing books. Walking with purpose. Living out miracles you did not even pray for. Every step you took, even the dumb ones, the dangerous ones, and the confused ones, had something holy guarding it.

Come on, somebody! I feel the Holy Ghost up in here!

"You listening? No... I mean REALLY listening?"

PROTECTION YOU NEVER SAW COMING

Let me tell you about the kind of protection I am talking about. Not the kind you see in movies where angels show up with swords and dramatic music. I am talking about the quiet kind. The invisible kind. The kind where you walk past danger and do not even know it was there. The kind where you make a decision that should have destroyed you, but God redirects it before it lands. The kind where you are about to step into a trap, and something in your spirit says, "Not today."

I am talking about the protection that kept you from getting in that car with that person. The protection that made you late to an appointment that would have put you in the wrong place at the wrong time. The protection that made you change your mind at the last second. The protection that gave you a bad feeling about something that turned out to be dangerous. The protection that kept you from saying yes to something that looked good but was really poison.

You know what I am talking about. Those moments where you look back and say, "If I had done that, I would not be here right now." Those moments where you realize God was protecting you from yourself. Those moments when you understand that your survival was not luck. It was divine intervention.

(The organist grins because they can FEEL what's coming.)

THE PROTECTION NOBODY TALKS ABOUT

Let me talk about the protection nobody talks about. The protection from the things you never saw. The accidents that almost happened but did not. The sicknesses that tried to attach to you but could not. The attacks that were planned against you but never reached you. The betrayals that were set up but God exposed before they could hurt you. The traps that were laid for you, but God dismantled before you got there.

You do not even know how many times God saved you from something you never saw coming. You do not even know how many times angels blocked something that had your name on it. You do not even know how many times God said, "Not this one. Not today. Not ever."

And that is the kind of protection that makes you want to shout. Not because you saw it. But because you KNOW it happened. You know it in your spirit. You know it in your bones. You know it in your soul. God has been protecting you from things you will never even know about.

(Pastor Paul points toward the sky like someone up there owes him an explanation.)

WHEN I REALIZED GOD WAS PROTECTING ME EVEN WHEN I WAS NOT PROTECTING MYSELF

This part right here is going to hit different. Because let me be honest. There were seasons in my life when I was not protecting myself. I was making bad decisions. I was ignoring red flags. I was walking into danger. I was trusting the wrong people. I was saying yes to things I should have said no to. I was saying no to things I should have said yes to. I was running from what I needed and running toward what would hurt me.

And you know what? God STILL protected me. Even when I was not protecting myself. Even when I was being foolish. Even when I was being stubborn. Even when I was being reckless. Even when I was being careless. God said, "I am going to protect him anyway. Because I know who he is going to become. I know what he is going to do. I know the purpose I put inside him. And I am not going to let his mistakes destroy what I am building."

That is the kind of love that makes you cry. That is the kind of grace that makes you grateful. That is the kind of mercy that makes you want to live right. Not because you have to. But because you WANT to. Because you realize God loved you enough to protect you even when you did not deserve it.

(The reader nods slowly.)

PUT A PIN IN IT RIGHT HERE

God's protection is not random. It is strategic, intentional, and purposeful. God did not protect your body, mind, heart, spirit, calling, future, and destiny just so you could survive. He protected you because SOMEBODY on earth needs the version of you that you are still becoming. You were not protected for comfort. You were protected for PURPOSE.

THE CANCER JOURNEY—WHEN PROTECTION LOOKED LIKE PRESENCE

Let me pull in another piece of my testimony. You remember the cancer. You remember the radiation room. You remember the smell, the cold air, and the fear in the pit of your stomach. You remember hearing words that shook your soul. You remember sitting in the doctor's office, trying to breathe when your whole world felt like it was holding its breath.

There were nights my body hurt in places I could not describe. Nights, I stayed strong for everybody else but felt empty as a drum inside. Nights when fear climbed on my chest at 2 am and whispered every worst-case scenario in my ear. Nights when I felt like the room was closing in slowly.

But guess what?

God was there.

Not metaphorically. Not symbolically. I mean **in the room**—sitting right in the middle of my crisis wearing a white coat and a Jamaican accent so thick it could heal you before the medicine did.

He showed up in the form of **Dr. Hayes**—my angel disguised as a man.

That wild, brilliant Jamaican doctor who refused to let death have the final say. He had the fire of the Caribbean sun in his spirit and the stubbornness of a prophet who dared anything that tried to take me out.

He was not just a doctor...

He was a *custodian of hope.*

When the textbooks ran out of answers, he did not.
When the charts said, "There is nothing more we can do," he rolled up his sleeves and said, **"Watch me."**

This man went beyond protocol, beyond comfort, beyond borders.
He flew all the way to **Africa** to find a new medication—not because it was required, but because he was determined that I would live long enough to tell this story.

Then he came back and administered that medicine with the care of an artist crafting a masterpiece—steady hands, fierce heart, holy purpose.

He was a guardian angel in the flesh.
A warrior who fought when I had no strength to lift my own hands.
A shield standing between me and the grave.

God was with me...

In the machine.
In the hallways.
In the waiting rooms.
In the tears nobody saw.
In the prayers I was too weak to pray.
In the silence where fear screamed the loudest.

And in those moments when all I had left was breath...
God protected THAT too.

I did not come out because I am lucky.
I came out because **I am marked.**
I am still here because heaven declared,
"This one finishes his assignment."

Come on, somebody! Let me say that again for somebody in the back row. You are still here because God has an assignment for you!

(The organ erupts like Pentecost round two.)

PROTECTION THROUGH THE GRIEF

Let me talk about another kind of protection. The protection through grief. When Mama went home. When Daddy went home. When the two people who gave me life were no longer here to walk with me through life. That kind of grief can kill you. Not physically. But spiritually. Emotionally. Mentally. That kind of grief can make you want to give up. That kind of grief can make you question everything. That kind of grief can make you wonder if you are going to make it.

But God protected me through that grief. He did not take the grief away. But He protected my mind from breaking under the weight of it. He protected my heart from closing permanently.

He protected my faith from dying with them. He protected my purpose from being buried with them. He protected my future from ending with their past.

And I know some of you reading this right now are walking through grief. You lost somebody. You lost something. You lost a dream. You lost a relationship. You lost a job. You lost your health. You lost your peace. You lost your hope. And you are wondering if you are going to make it through this.

Let me tell you something. God is protecting you right now. Even in the grief. Even in the pain. Even in the loss. Even in the heartbreak. He is protecting your mind. He is protecting your heart. He is protecting your faith. He is protecting your purpose. He is protecting your future. You are going to make it through this. Not because you are strong. But because God is protecting you.

THE ENEMY TRIED IT, BUT GOD BLOCKED IT EVERY TIME

Let me make this plain. If the enemy could have killed you, you would be dead. Let that sink in. The fact that you are reading this, breathing, thinking, processing, hoping, and healing is PROOF that the enemy FAILED.

He tried depression. FAILED. He tried sickness. FAILED. He tried grief. FAILED. He tried fear. FAILED. He tried trauma. FAILED. He tried heartbreak. FAILED. He tried the wrong people. FAILED. He tried low self-esteem. FAILED. He tried loneliness. FAILED. He tried shame. FAILED. He tried confusion. FAILED. He tried exhaustion. FAILED. He tried old habits. FAILED. He tried cancer. FAILED. He tried your childhood wounds. FAILED. He tried your darkest night. FAILED.

Your survival is not subtle. Your survival is not delicate. Your survival is not background noise. Your survival is a head-on collision between Hell's intention and Heaven's intervention. Hell had a plan. Heaven had a PURPOSE. And purpose won.

(Pastor Paul clutches his chest.)

PROTECTION IN THE SMALL THINGS

Let me talk about the protection of the small things. The things you do not even think about. The protection that kept you from getting sick when everybody around you was sick. The protection that kept your car running when it should have broken down. The protection that kept your mind clear when stress should have clouded it. The protection that kept your bills paid when the math did not make sense. The protection that kept your relationships intact when they should have fallen apart.

God is not just protecting you from the big things. He is protecting you in the small stuff, too. Every day. Every hour. Every minute. Every second. He is watching over you. He is guarding you. He is covering you. He is keeping you. And most of the time, you do not even notice. But it is happening. All the time. Every single day.

MY DECLARATION—AND YOURS

Stand in this moment like it is an altar call. Straighten your back. Lift your head. Open your heart. Take a breath. And declare with your FULL soul, "God has protected me from things I will NEVER know about."

Say it again till your spirit stands tall. "He kept me from evil. He kept my soul. He kept my mind. He kept my purpose. He kept my steps. And He is STILL keeping me."

Now stretch your hands out like you are handing out deliverance at a revival and declare with authority, "THANK YOU, LORD, for every step You protected."

Because if He had not? You would not be reading this book. You would not be alive. You would not be whole. You would not be here. But you ARE here. Not by accident. Not by coincidence. Not by luck. You are here because God walked beside you, in front of you, and behind you EVERY SINGLE STEP.

(The organ takes off like it's chasing glory itself.)

"OHHHHH JESUS!"
I'M ABOUT TO WHOOOOOP LIKE I OWE GOD
PRAISE FROM MY GUTS!

Let me close this chapter like a REAL preacher! When I think
about ALL the steps I took that should have destroyed me, ALL
the moments that should have ended me, ALL the storms that
should have drowned me, ALL the people that should have
broken me, ALL the decisions that should have wrecked me,
ALL the sickness that should have taken me out, ALL the grief
that should have buried me alive, ALL the danger that should
have killed me, and yet, I AM. STILL. HERE!

My soul goes into PRAISE mode! And I shout with EVERY
ounce of breath in me, "THANK YOU, LORD! YOU HAVE
BEEN MY PROTECTION EVERY STEP OF THE WAY!"

He kept me! He covered me! He carried me! He guided me! He
lifted me! He rescued me! He restored me! He rebuilt me! He
surrounded me! He held me when nothing else could hold me!

Somebody lift your hands right now because God put a body-
guard on your life, and you did not even know his name! Somebody shout right now because angels have been working over-

time protecting you! Somebody praise right now because you should have been gone, but God said, "NOT THIS ONE!"

And if you KNOW that is your story too, then lift your voice and shout, "THANK YOU, LORD, FOR PROTECTING ME!"

You walked through fire and did not burn! You walked through water and did not drown! You walked through valleys and did not die! You walked through storms and did not break! You walked through hell and came out WHOLE!

THANK YOU, LORD! THANK YOU, LORD! THANK YOU, LORD!

Welcome deeper into the journey. Chapter 6 is waiting. And trust me, it is about to get even more powerful.

Chapter 6

It Wasn't the Alarm—It Was Mercy

God Gave Me This Day

S **CRIPTURE**

Lamentations 3:22-23 (KJV): "It is of the Lord's mercies that we are not consumed... They are new every morning: great is thy faithfulness."

Lamentations 3:22-23 (PASTOR PAUL'S Translation): "I wake up because God restocks the shelf of mercy every morning. Fresh grace. Fresh strength. Fresh power. Fresh breath. Fresh hope. Fresh purpose. He keeps me going when I do not even know how I am going. He renews what I thought was empty. He refills what I thought was finished. And He does it EVERY SINGLE MORNING without me even asking."

(The organ creeps in soft, like a mighty rushing wind on tiptoe.)

Let me start this one by walking into the pulpit with a limp, a testimony, and a handful of survival stories I have never told out loud. This chapter right here? This is the "let me catch my breath" chapter. The "Lord, if You do nothing else, thank You for THIS" chapter. The one that makes you close the book, lean back in your chair, look up at the ceiling, and whisper, "God, You really kept me."

Because Chapter 6 is not about miracles. This one is not about storms. It is not even about the devil. This chapter is about the quiet moments, the everyday mercies, the daily resurrections, and the mornings you woke up and did not even know THAT was the miracle.

Let me tell you where this chapter began for me. It was a morning when I woke up tired. Not sleepy tired. I am talking tired, tired. The tired where your bones sigh. Your eyelids protest. Your spirit leans over and says, "Brother, not today."

My room was dark, but not peaceful-dark. More like "God, can You send help?" dark. I sat on the edge of my bed, hunched over like I was the extra in a Tyler Perry drama, and I whispered, "Lord, I do not have it today."

And right there, in my exhaustion, in my weakness, in my empty tank, I felt the Lord whisper back, "Good. Use Mine."

(Pastor Paul stops, grips the podium, and tilts his whole head sideways.)

WHEW. That hit me so hard I had to sit still and let it settle. Because that was the revelation of my LIFE. I have never kept myself going. God has been carrying me. Through cancer. Through fear. Through grief. Through disappointment. Through the nights where the room spun and the tears came without permission. Through the mornings, I woke up feeling like my purpose was on life support.

I did not make it through radiation on willpower. God kept me. I did not make it through losing Mama and Daddy on strength. God kept me. I did not make it through the anxiety, the financial stress, the pressure of ministry, the disappointment of people, or the brokenness of being the "strong one" in discipline. God kept me.

And the truth? He kept me EVERY DAY. Not occasionally. Not when I remembered to pray. Not when I behaved right. Not when I felt strong. Every. Single. Day.

"Ohhhhhh wait... wait... somethin' breaking loose!"

I HAVE BEEN LIVING ON BORROWED STRENGTH

You know what I realized sitting on that bed? I have been living on borrowed strength. Grace strength. Mercy strength. God's strength. Strength God restocks every morning like divine Amazon Prime. Because every day I wake up is proof that God renewed something inside me while I was asleep.

And that is why this chapter matters. Because you do not praise God right until you realize it was not your alarm clock that woke you up. It was mercy. Fresh. Refilled. Rebooted. Restocked. Every morning.

And I do not know about you, but I have had too many days when I woke up running on fumes, pretending I have been self-sustaining. I am a kept man. Kept by grace. Kept by mercy. Kept by strength I did not earn. Kept by air I did not pay for. Kept by power I did not generate. Kept by a God who refuses to let me fall apart permanently.

Come on, somebody! I feel the Holy Ghost up in here!

THIS CHAPTER IS ABOUT THE EVERYDAY THINGS

This chapter is not about the big things. It is about the everyday things, the quiet miracles, the subtle mercies, the invisible protections, the strength that shows up on days you forgot to ask for it. It is about the truth you do not want to admit. You would be dead, drained, depressed, or done if God did not keep you EVERY DAY.

Let me walk you through the days you had no energy, the mornings you woke up broken, the tears nobody saw, the exhaustion that felt spiritual, the moments you almost gave up, the Holy Ghost power that carried you anyway, the times God preserved your mind, the mercy that met you before your feet hit the floor, the grace that renewed itself when you did not, and the strength God poured into you when you were running on negative.

And by the end of this chapter, you will look at your life and say with your whole chest, "EVERY DAY BY YOUR POWER, YOU KEEP ON KEEPING ME."

(Pastor Paul rocks back and forth like he's fighting the shout.)

THAT MORNING, WHEN I WOKE UP TIRED, AND GOD SAID, "USE MY STRENGTH"

Let me set the scene. It was one of those mornings where the air felt heavy. The room was quiet. Not peaceful and quiet. More like "something is about to shift" quietly. I opened my eyes and immediately felt the weight. The weight of everything I had been carrying. The weight of grief. The weight of responsibility. The weight of being strong for everybody else. The weight of ministry. The weight of expectations. The weight of survival.

And I sat there on the edge of my bed, hunched over, head in my hands, and I said out loud, "Lord, I do not have it today. I do not have the strength. I do not have the energy. I do not have the words. I do not have the faith. I do not have the courage. I do not have it."

And God said, "Good. Because I do. Use Mine."

That is when I realized something that changed my entire perspective. I have been trying to run on my own strength when God has been offering me His the whole time. I have been trying to carry burdens he never asked me to carry. I have been trying to be strong when He was offering to be strong FOR me.

(The organ trembles higher.)

THE MORNINGS I WOKE UP AND DID NOT WANT TO

Let me be honest. There were mornings I woke up and did not want to. I did not want to face the day. I did not want to deal with the pain. I did not want to carry the weight. I did not want to be strong. I did not want to smile. I did not want to pretend. I did not want to fight. I did not want to hope. I did not want to believe. I did not want to try.

But something in me, something I did not put there, something holy, something divine, something supernatural, said, "Get up anyway." And I did. Not because I wanted to. But because God gave me the strength to do what I did not want to do.

That is the kind of power I am talking about. The kind that shows up when you have nothing left. The kind that carries you when you cannot carry yourself. The kind that moves you when you are too tired to move. The kind that breathes for you when you forget how to breathe.

Come on, somebody! Let me say that again for somebody in the back row. God gives you the strength to do what you do not want to do!

PUT A PIN IN IT RIGHT HERE

Every morning you wake up is not just a new day. It is new mercy. It is new grace. It is new strength. It is new power. It is new hope. It is new purpose. God does not just give you life. He gives you the ability to LIVE that life. And He does it EVERY SINGLE DAY without you even asking.

THE DAYS I CRIED BEFORE BREAKFAST

Let me talk about the days I cried before breakfast. The days where the tears came before the coffee. The days when grief woke up before I did. The days when pain was the first thing I felt when I opened my eyes. The days when I had to cry it out before I could face it.

Those were the days when God's mercy was most evident. Because on those days, I had nothing. No strength. No courage. No faith. No hope. Nothing. But God gave me just enough to make it through. Just enough to get out of bed. Just enough to take a shower. Just enough to get dressed. Just enough to face the day. Just enough to survive.

And you know what? Just enough was enough. Because God does not give you strength for the whole week. He gives you strength for the day. He does not give you grace for the entire month. He gives you grace for the moment. He does not give you power for the entire year. He gives you control of the step.

(The reader sits straight up like revival just entered the room.)

WHEN CANCER TRIED TO WRITE MY LAST CHAPTER

Let me talk about when cancer tried to write my last chapter. When I sat in that doctor's office and heard words that shook my soul. When I walked into that radiation room, I felt fear grip my chest. When I laid on that table and wondered if I was going to make it through this.

I was sitting in my car, too tired to drive, too scared to cry, too overwhelmed to speak. I said, "Lord, I do not feel like a miracle today." And God whispered, "Feelings do not keep you. I do."

Right there in that parking lot, in that moment of fear and weakness, God carried me again. Not because I was brave. Not because I was positive. Not because I was strong. But because God REFUSED to let cancer write the last chapter of my life. He said, "You are not done. I am keeping you until the work is finished."

And that is why this chapter matters. Because even when you do not understand why you are still here, God does.

(The organ breaks into a double-time praise run.)

WHEN YOU WAKE UP TIRED BUT STILL MAKE IT THROUGH THE DAY—THAT IS GOD

Let me talk to the grown folks. The ones who carry entire worlds quietly. The ones who do not get days off from responsibility. The ones who push through pain because people depend on them. You know what it is like to wake up tired and STILL make it through a day that should have broken you.

That is not you. That is God. He kept your sanity, courage, breath, dignity, patience, peace, compassion, hope, identity, and purpose. He kept your mind from folding. He kept your emotions from exploding. He kept your heart from dissolving. He kept your life from collapsing.

Every time you said, "I cannot do this," God answered, "Yes, you can. Because I am doing it THROUGH you."

Come on, somebody! Ask your neighbor, "Did God keep you today?"

THE PART WHERE YOUR SOUL SAYS "THANK YOU" WITHOUT YOUR MOUTH SPEAKING

There are days when gratitude shows up without language. Your soul bows. Your spirit hums. Your chest warms. And something in you whispers without words, "Thank You for keeping me."

You cannot always articulate it. You cannot always explain it. You cannot always testify about it. But your SOUL knows. God kept you in places you never should have survived. He kept you in seasons that were supposed to break you. He kept you in storms that should have drowned you. He kept you in grief that should have swallowed you. He kept you through fear that should have paralyzed you. He kept you through trauma that should have erased you.

Your soul remembers EVERYTHING God did, even when your mind forgets.

(Pastor Paul slaps his knee.)

GOD'S MORNING MERCY IS THE REASON YOU ARE STILL ALIVE

Let me tell you something heavy but healing. If God ever stopped giving you mercy, even for one morning, you would not survive the day. Not with everything you have survived. Not with the weight you carry. Not with the trauma you have endured. Not with the exhaustion you have pushed through. Not with the secrets you have held. Not with the grief that sits in your bones.

If God did not renew mercy DAILY? Your spirit would have collapsed. Your mind would have broken. Your body would have given up. Your joy would have evaporated. Your hope would have turned to dust.

But look at you. Still standing. Still breathing. Still fighting. Still growing. Still dreaming. Still becoming. Why? Because God refuses to let your story end before its time. Every morning you wake up is Heaven's way of saying, "I STILL have plans for you."

SOMETIMES GOD'S POWER SHOWS UP IN THE SMALLEST WAYS

We love big miracles, the red-sea-splitting, fire-falling, mountain-moving kind. But the older I get, the wiser I become, the more life I have lived, and the more I realize that small mercies are sometimes the biggest miracles.

Small things like the breath you did not have to think about, the peace that did not make sense, the smile that fought its way back, the strength you did not ask for, the idea that came out of nowhere, the moment your anxiety calmed itself, the unexpected encouragement, the random clarity, the feeling of "I got one more day in me," the tears that finally fell, the laughter that surprised you, the nap that healed your soul, the text that reminded you you are loved, the memory that made you grateful, and the Holy Ghost hug that came at the perfect time.

These are not "little things." These are God things. These are the daily reminders that His power does not just show up in storms. It shows up in survival.

WHEN YOU LOOK BACK, YOU WILL SEE GOD'S FINGERPRINTS ON EVERY DAY

I dare you to look back, not at the pain, not at the mistakes, not at the failures, not at the trauma, but at the THREAD. The thread of mercy. The thread of strength. The thread of protection. The thread of grace. The thread of "you made it when you should not have." The thread of "you kept going even when you did not want to." The thread of "God stepped in again."

When you look back, you will truly see that God did not just show up in the big moments. He showed up EVERY DAY. In the cancer diagnosis. In the radiation room. In the grief of losing Mama and Daddy. In the storm of fear that followed you. In the pressure of ministry. In the exhaustion of being the strong one. In the quiet nights where tears had to do the talking. In the moments you did not know how to pray. In the mornings, you woke up tired but still got up. In the decisions you did not think you could make. In the path you did not know you could walk.

Every page of your life has God's fingerprints on it. Every chapter. Every line. Every step. Every breath.

(The organ hums powerful.)

"He KEPT me in secret places!"
IMMA WHOOOOOP LIKE MY SURVIVAL IS A PSALM!

(The organ explodes into full praise mode.)

Let me close this chapter the ONLY way it deserves! My God! When I think about the MERCY that met me every morning! When I think about the GRACE that carried me every day! When I think about the POWER that held me when I should have fallen! When I think about the STRENGTH that was not mine but kept me alive anyway! My soul gets LOUD!

Because I remember the days I woke up weak, but God made me strong! I remember the mornings I woke up empty, but God filled me again! I remember the weeks I cried myself to sleep, but God dried my tears before sunrise! I remember the nights the cancer fear tried to break me, but God whispered, "You will LIVE and not die!" I remember the morning grief tried to sit on my chest, but God said, "Get up. My mercy is already here!" I remember the seasons where I thought I was finished, but God said, "Your story is not done!"

And so today, with everything in me, I declare, "EVERY DAY BY YOUR POWER, YOU KEEP ON KEEPING ME!"

He kept me through storms! He kept me through sickness! He kept me through fear! He kept me through grief! He kept me through loss! He kept me through exhaustion! He kept me through anger! He kept me through heartbreak! He kept me in confusion! He kept me through depression! He kept me through trauma! And He is STILL keeping me!

Somebody lift your hands right now because your alarm clock did not wake you up this morning; MERCY DID! Somebody shout right now because you are not running on your own strength; you are running on GOD'S POWER! Somebody praise right now because every day you wake up is proof that God renewed something in you while you were sleeping!

So I shout it with my whole chest: THANK YOU, LORD, FOR MERCY EVERY MORNING! THANK YOU, LORD, FOR POWER EVERY DAY! THANK YOU, LORD, FOR KEEPING ME WHEN I COULD NOT KEEP MYSELF!

Every day! Every hour! Every moment! HE KEEPS ME!

THANK YOU, LORD! THANK YOU, LORD! THANK YOU, LORD!

Welcome deeper into the journey. Chapter 7 is waiting. And trust me, it is about to get even more powerful.

He Saved Me Before, but He's Still Saving Me Now

That's Why My Praise Stays Loud

SCRIPTURE

Psalm 46:1 (KJV): "God is our refuge and strength, a very present help in trouble."

Psalm 46:1 (PASTOR PAUL'S Translation): "When trouble shows up, God does not call ahead, text back later, or send you to voicemail. He shows up immediately, WITH power, WITH love, and WITH protection, every hour on the hour. He does not wait for you to get your life together. He does not wait for you to deserve it. He does not wait for you to ask nicely. He just SHOWS UP."

(The organ warms up like Sunday morning before sunrise.)

Let me set the scene. Because Chapter 7 is not just a chapter. It is a confession, a testimony, a moment of clarity, and a public declaration that I have survived WAY too many "almosts" for God not to get ALL this praise.

Have you ever sat down somewhere, in a quiet room, a living room, a car, a kitchen table, or a couch that leans like it needs prayer, and suddenly all your "almosts" come rushing back? The almost car accident. The almost heartbreak that would have broken your whole life. The almost sickness that could have changed your destiny. The depression that almost swallowed you whole. The danger you ALMOST walked into because you were being hardheaded. The relationship you almost married into, Lord have mercy, that would have taken you out quicker than a poorly cooked potluck dish.

Yeah. This chapter starts right there.

(Pastor Paul looks over the congregation like he sees every struggle they hiding.)

THE DAY MY "ALMOSTS" CAME BACK FOR A MEETING

It was not even a dramatic day. It was not a thunderstorm. It was not a funeral. It was not a hospital room. Nah. I was sitting on my couch, the same couch I have been threatening to replace since Bill Clinton was in office, and I had one of those moments where everything got quiet. And it hit me HARD.

"Paul, you are only alive because God kept blocking things."

And I am not talking about the cute things. I am talking about the BIG ones. That diagnosis the doctor was scared to mention. That pressure in your chest you ignored because you had things to do. That reckless season where you were running from yourself and running into danger at the same time. That betrayal should have destroyed your Heart permanently. That depression that tried to bury you. That night, you cried till your lungs hurt, and God stepped in like, "Not today. I am still keeping you."

That moment you almost made a permanent decision in a temporary storm. That time, grief almost swallowed you after losing the people you love. That time, fear almost convinced you to give up on writing, preaching, singing, and living.

"Don't you dare blink... don't you miss this moment!"

And then there are the OTHER "almosts." The ones you do not talk about in church. The ones you survived, even though it was nothing but grace covering your behind. You know the ones. The relationship you knew was not God; you were bored, and they smelled nice. The argument that almost took you to jail. The text message that would have resurrected disaster from the dead. The decision you almost made because pride was driving and wisdom had exited the vehicle.

The places you had NO BUSINESS being in, but God sent something to stop you. A flat tire. A dead phone. A friend calling at the right moment. A sudden headache. A weird vibe. A Holy Ghost, "do not you dare."

And the worst one? The moment you almost gave up on yourself.

Whew. I sat there staring at the wall like the wall owed me rent money, and I said out loud, "God, You really protected me from EVERYTHING. The enemy. People. Life. And me."

And I swear, for a second, it felt like the whole room whispered back, "Every hour."

Come on, somebody! I feel the Holy Ghost up in here!

PERSONAL TRUTH TIME

I do not mind telling you the truth. There were seasons I was not wise. I was not careful. I was not listening. I was not praying. I was not discerning. I was not paying attention. I was not even TRYING to be kept. But somehow, I was still kept.

Through cancer. Through fear. Through heartbreak. Through depression. Through loneliness. Through stupid choices I made with confidence. Through moments, I did not think I would make it to the next morning.

I survived things that other people did not. I walked out of seasons that other people never recovered from. I kept breathing through storms that tried to shut my lungs down. And when I could not walk? God carried me like somebody's spoiled grandbaby. When I could not pray? God prayed over me. When I could not think straight? God held my mind together with heavenly duct tape. When I could not see my worth? He hid me from people who would have destroyed me. When I did not even WANT protection? He covered me anyway.

That is when I realized. God does not protect me because I am good. He protects me because HE is good.

(The organ takes a deep, soulful inhale.)

THE REVELATION THAT BUILT THIS WHOLE CHAPTER

Here it is. God has been showing up for me EVERY HOUR, protecting me from danger, from disaster, from people, from trauma, from attack, from failure, from heartbreak, from sickness, from foolishness, from fear, and from MYSELF.

He did not show up monthly. He did not show up seasonally. He did not show up annually. He did not show up "when I deserved it." He showed up EVERY. SINGLE. HOUR.

And THAT is the whole energy of this chapter. This is not just gratitude. This is not just testimony. This is not just a reflection. This is me standing flat-footed in my truth, saying, "God, You protected me as Your life depended on it." Because He loves me. Because He sees purpose in me. Because He refuses to let my story end before it is finished.

(Pastor Paul pulls the mic close like he about to tell heaven's secrets.)

LOVE THAT PROTECTS EVEN WHEN YOU DO NOT DESERVE IT

Let me talk about the kind of love that protects you even when you do not deserve it. The type of love that covers you even when you are being foolish. The kind of love that shields you even when you are walking into danger with your eyes wide open. The kind of love that says, "I am going to protect you anyway because I know who you are going to become."

That is the kind of love God has for you. Not the kind that waits for you to get it right. Not the kind that waits for you to deserve it. Not the kind that waits for you to earn it. The kind that shows up BEFORE you even know you need it. The kind that blocks things BEFORE they even get to you. The kind that covers you BEFORE the attack even happens.

Come on, somebody! Let me say that again for somebody in the back row. God protects you BEFORE you even know you need protection!

POWER THAT SHOWS UP IN YOUR WEAKNESS

Let me talk about the power that shows up in your weakness. The power that carries you when you cannot carry yourself. The power that holds you when you are falling apart. The power that strengthens you when you have nothing left. The power that lifts you when you cannot stand. The power that moves you when you are too tired to move.

I am talking about the power that showed up in that radiation room. The power that showed up in that hospital bed. The power that showed up in that dark room when I was crying. The power that showed up in that moment when I wanted to give up. The power that showed up in that season when I thought I was finished.

That power did not wait for me to be strong. That power showed up IN my weakness. That power did not wait for me to have faith. That power showed up IN my doubt. That power did not wait for me to be ready. That power showed up IN my brokenness.

(The reader's spirit starts pacing even if their body ain't.)

PROTECTION THAT LOOKS LIKE CLOSED DOORS

Let me talk about the protection that looks like closed doors. The protection that looks like rejection. The protection that looks like disappointment. The protection appears to be a loss. Because sometimes God's protection does not look like protection. Sometimes it seems like heartbreak.

God will let someone walk out because He sees the REAL them. God will make someone ghost you because He heard conversations you did not. God will shut down a relationship because He saw the crash coming. God will break what YOU called "meant to be" because He knew it was going to break YOU.

Looking back, there are people I cried over that I should have thrown a party for leaving. There are doors I begged God to open that God had already labeled "hazard zone." There are opportunities I wanted that would have ruined my mind, money, and ministry. There are friendships I thought were forever that were actually seasonal, and God ended the season for my protection.

And you know what I realized? Every rejection was a rescue. Every closed door was a covering. Every "no" was divine CPR on my destiny. That is protection. Every hour.

(The organ trembles.)

PUT A PIN IN IT RIGHT HERE

God does not protect what He does not plan to use. Protection is not random. Protection is intentional. Protection is strategic. Protection is love in action. Protection is heaven refusing to lose you. If God has gone out of His way to shield you from death, heartbreak, mistakes, sickness, danger, disaster, betrayal, depression, and yourself, it means He has plans for you that hell cannot interfere with. Protection is proof of purpose.

ME TALKING TO MY OWN HEART

One night, I put my hand on my chest, right in the middle of old grief, old heartbreak, and old disappointment, and I said, "Heart, look at you. You are still beating."

And my Heart beat like it knew something I did not. Lub-dub. Lub-dub. Lub-dub. Steady. Not fast. Not panicked. Not breaking. Steady.

And I heard God whisper, "I protected your heart when life tried to stop it."

I wanted to cry. Because I knew the truth. I survived heartbreak that should have made me bitter. I survived grief that should have paralyzed me. I survived seasons I had no strength to walk through. I survived myself. And that, THAT, is protection.

Come on, somebody! Ask your neighbor, "Did God protect your heart too?"

THE DANGERS GOD CANCELED

If every trap that was set for you, if every plan meant to destroy you, if every lie meant to break you, if every attack meant to crush you, if every scheme that had your name on it had reached you, let me tell you something. You would not be here. Not reading. Not breathing. Not healing. Not dreaming. Not writing books. Not building your life back. Not becoming the version of you that destiny requires.

The ONLY reason you are still here is that God stood in front of things you did not even know were coming. That is love. That is power. That is protection. EVERY HOUR.

There is a WHOLE SUPERNATURAL FILE with your name on it titled "DANGERS GOD CANCELED." Underneath that? "Foolishness You Walked Into." Underneath THAT? "Mercy Interventions." And the folder is THICK.

(Pastor Paul starts the preacher rock.)

THE PRAISE THAT COMES FROM REAL SURVIVORS

Have you ever wondered why your praise has depth now? Because it is layered with "I should not even be alive." "I should not be this sane." "I should not be recovering this well." "I should not be walking into this season." "I should not be this blessed." "I should not have this joy." "I should not still have a calling." "I should not have gotten another chance." "I should not have been spared." "I should not have survived ME."

Your praise is not cosplay. Your praise is not performance. Your praise is not practice. Your praise is PROOF. Because you KNOW. If God had not stepped in? If God had not intervened? If God had not interfered? If God had not blocked it? If God had not covered you? If God had not shielded you? You would not be here.

THE FINAL DECLARATION—YOUR TURN TO SAY IT

Place your hand on your chest. Take a deep breath. Slow. Steady. Feel that life? Now say this with your FULL chest. "God, thank You for loving me stronger than I knew how to love myself."

Say it again. "Thank You for Your POWER, the power that held me when I was not holdable."

Say it louder. "Thank You for protecting me EVERY HOUR from danger, from people, from life, and from my own decisions."

And now the final declaration, the one that breaks things off from your past and unlocks your next level. "LOVE. POWER. PROTECTION. EVERY HOUR. AND THAT IS WHY I AM STILL HERE."

Because the truth is simple. You did not keep yourself. God kept you. Every hour. Every minute. Every moment. And He is STILL keeping you.

(The organist modulates like they trying to tear the roof off.)

(The organ trembles.)

(Pastor Paul lunges back from the mic.)

"OHHHHHHH MY GOD!"

I'M 'BOUT TO WHOOOOOP LIKE HE SURROUNDED MY STEPS!

(The organ shakes like a heartbeat of revival.)

Let me close this chapter the way it deserves to be closed! When I think about all the "almosts" in my life! When I think about all the dangers God blocked! When I think about all the traps He dismantled! When I think about all the attacks He intercepted! When I think about all the heartbreaks He prevented! When I think about all the disasters He canceled! My soul goes into PRAISE mode!

Because God did not just save me once! He saves me EVERY SINGLE HOUR! He does not just protect me sometimes! He protects me ALL THE TIME! He does not just love me when I am good! He loves me EVERY HOUR!

Somebody lift your hands right now because God has been showing up for you EVERY HOUR! Somebody shout right now because His love has been covering you EVERY HOUR! Somebody praise right now because His power has been holding you EVERY HOUR! Somebody worship right now because His protection has been shielding you EVERY HOUR!

And if you KNOW this chapter is your story too, then lift your voice and say, "THANK YOU, LORD, FOR LOVE, POWER, AND PROTECTION EVERY HOUR!"

You should have been gone, but God said, "NOT THIS ONE!" You should have been broken, but God said, "I AM KEEPING THIS ONE!" You should have been destroyed, but God said, "I HAVE PLANS FOR THIS ONE!"

LOVE. POWER. PROTECTION. EVERY HOUR!

THANK YOU, LORD! THANK YOU, LORD! THANK YOU, LORD!

Welcome to the final chapter. Chapter 8 is waiting. And trust me, it is about to bring everything home.

Chapter 8

I Open My Mouth to Thank Him—But I End Up Dancing

I Owe God Too Much To Whisper

SCRIPTURE

Psalm 103:1-2 (KJV): "Bless the LORD, O my soul: and all that is within me, bless his holy name. Bless the LORD, O my soul, and forget not all his benefits."

Psalm 103:1-2 (PASTOR PAUL'S Translation): "Everything in me, EVERYTHING, needs to stand up right now and bless God. My mind, my heart, my spirit, my memories, my scars, my survival, my breath, my purpose—ALL OF IT needs to give Him glory. And do not you dare forget what He did for you. Do not forget the healing. Do not forget the deliverance. Do not forget the protection. Do not forget the mercy. Do not forget the grace. Do not forget that you should not be here, but you ARE."

(The organ hums low like thunder rolling across a valley.)

Let me tell you something before we even open this chapter all the way. This one is not written with my pen. This one is written from my SURVIVAL. This is not polished. This is not cute. This is not poetic. This is a raw, unfiltered, straight-off-the-battlefield chapter.

Because when I reached THIS part of the book and THIS part of my life, God would not even let me write standing up. He said, "Sit down, Paul. Let us go through what I brought you through."

And when we started walking through it, when we started unpacking the last seven chapters of my LIFE, my chest got tight, my eyes got hot, and my soul whispered the loudest truth I had. THANK YOU, LORD, for ALL You have done for me.

(Pastor Paul wipes his forehead, then wipes it AGAIN, then looks at the towel like it betrayed him.)

THE DAY ALL MY SURVIVAL STORIES COLLIDED AT ONCE

It was a quiet day. Not a church day. Not a dramatic day. Not a stormy day. A regular day, sitting in my living room, on that old, tired couch that has seen more tears than some churches, and all of a sudden, my whole life flashed back at me.

But not the pretty parts. Not the proud parts. Not the "Instagram testimony" parts. No, the real stuff. The hidden stuff. The unspoken stuff. The almost died stuff. The almost quit stuff. The almost-lost-my-mind stuff.

The cancer diagnosis. The grief that washed over me after losing my parents. The nights I cried until my ribs hurt. The seasons I smiled through depression because "I am strong." The times danger tried to take me out in the streets of D.C. The relationships that would have DESTROYED me if God had not stepped in. The fear that kept me from writing books I was BORN to write. The shame, the guilt, the memories, the mistakes—everything came back at once.

And instead of collapsing, instead of breaking, instead of folding under the weight of all I survived, my spirit STOOD UP inside me like an old Black church mother and said, "THANK YOU, LORD, for all You have done for me."

(Pastor Paul wipes sweat.)

Come on, somebody! I feel the Holy Ghost up in here!

THE MOMENT GOD SHOWED ME THE "ALMOSTS" I HAD FORGOTTEN

Let me tell you something. God has a way of rewinding your life like a movie trailer, but He does not show you the glamorous scenes. No. He shows you the "that should have killed me" moment, the "I had no business surviving that" moment, the "I was one decision away from disaster" moment, the "I almost married the WRONG person" moment, the "I almost lost my life to depression" moment, the "I almost did not make it through that diagnosis" moment, the "I almost stayed stuck in grief forever" moment, and the "I almost gave up on my calling" moment.

And every time one of those "almosts" flashed before me, I felt God whisper, "I kept you. I protected you. I preserved you. I carried you. I hid you. I held you together when you were breaking."

And right there, in that living room, I realized. Everything that did not kill me became a reason to THANK HIM.

(The organist hollers, "TAKE YOUR TIME, PASTOR!")

THE DAY I REALIZED MY PRAISE WAS NOT A CHOICE—IT WAS A NECESSITY

Listen. I do not praise God because I am churchy. I do not praise because I am emotional. I do not praise because it sounds deep. I praise because cancer did not win, grief did not bury me, heartbreak did not destroy me, mistakes did not define me, trauma did not kill me, depression did not drown me, fear did not stop me, danger did not catch me, foolishness did not expose me, the enemy did not claim me, my past did not trap me, my own decisions did not take me out, and the devil did not get the last word.

How can I NOT thank Him?

My THANK YOU is not quiet. My THANK YOU is not polite. My THANK YOU is not professional. My THANK YOU is a SURVIVOR'S SHOUT. My THANK YOU is the sound of somebody who saw death, saw heartbreak, saw sickness, saw loss, saw fear, and saw darkness, and STILL lived.

My THANK YOU is my PRAISE because my survival is my testimony.

(Pastor Paul starts that old-school preacher rock — heel-to-toe shuffle!)

THE MOMENT GOD SAID, "NOW PRAISE ME FOR THE STUFF YOU DO NOT EVEN KNOW ABOUT"

Whew, let THIS sit in your chest. God said, "You are shouting over what you SAW, but you do not even know the half of what I BLOCKED."

The accidents He prevented. The sickness that never reached me. The heartbreak that never happened. The disaster that never formed. The people who meant me harm but never got access.

The breakdown I never had. The bullet I never saw. The car that never hit me. The diagnosis that never landed. The depression that did not drown me. The fear that did not swallow me. The shame that did not silence me. The trap that did not catch me. The night that did not kill me.

And I whispered out loud, "God, THANK YOU for the miracles I did not even know to pray for."

Because sometimes the greatest blessing is the danger you NEVER saw because God snatched it away first.

Come on, somebody! Let me say that again for somebody in the back row. God blocked things you never even saw coming!

WHEN YOUR GRATITUDE BECOMES A WEAPON

Before I even step into this chapter fully, let me tell you something straight. Your praise is not a church accessory. Your praise is EVIDENCE. Your praise is PROOF. Your praise is a WEAPON.

I am talking about the kind of praise that grows in the dark. The kind of praise that is born in hospital rooms. The kind of praise that survived funerals. The kind that did not die during the depression. The kind you whispered into your pillow when you did not want anybody to hear you cry.

This chapter? This is not Thanksgiving. This is not cute-sounding worship. This is SURVIVOR PRAISE. Let me say that again so your spirit catches it. MY THANK YOU IS MY PRAISE because my survival is my testimony.

This is thankfulness with a limp. With a scar. With a tear. With a story. This is gratitude from somebody who has been through SOMETHING.

(The reader stands in their spirit.)

THE PRAISE THAT WAS BORN IN MY DARKEST MOMENTS

Let me talk like I feel it. My praise did not come from the easy days. It did not come from the paychecks. It did not come from the victories. My THANK YOU was born in the cancer diagnosis, the radiation room, the nights my body hurt but my faith held on, the waiting rooms where fear whispered lies, the mornings I woke up tired but still got up, the seasons where I smiled through pain, and the moments where I had to choose between giving up and getting up.

That is where my praise was born. In the valley. In the fire. In the storm. In the darkness. In the pain. In fear. In the grief. In the struggle. That is where I learned to say THANK YOU.

Not because everything was good. But because God was GOOD in everything.

(The organ buzzes low.)

PUT A PIN IN IT RIGHT HERE

Your praise is not about what you have. Your praise is about what you survived. Your thank you is not about your blessings. Your thank you is about your battles. And if God brought you through something that should have destroyed you, your gratitude is not optional. It is MANDATORY. Because every time you open your mouth to say thank you, you are reminding hell that it FAILED.

WHEN I REALIZED MY SURVIVAL WAS MY MINISTRY

At some point, I realized something powerful. My survival is not just for me. My healing is not just for me. My deliverance is not just for me. My breakthrough is not just for me. My testimony is not just for me.

God kept me so I could tell somebody else, "You can make it too." God healed me so I could tell somebody else, "Healing is possible." God delivered me so I could tell somebody else, "You are not stuck." God brought me through so I could tell somebody else, "There is life after this."

My survival became my ministry. My scars became my sermon. My pain became my platform. My test became my testimony. My mess became my message.

And that is when I understood. God did not just save me. He saved me FOR something. He saved me FOR someone. He saved me FOR a purpose.

Come on, somebody! Ask your neighbor, "What is God saving you FOR?"

THE PRAISE THAT WILL NOT STAY QUIET

Let me tell you something about praise that comes from survival. It will not stay quiet. It will not stay seated. It will not stay calm. It will not stay contained. It will not stay professional. It will not stay polite.

Because when you know what God brought you through, when you know what He saved you from, when you know what He delivered you out of, when you know what He healed you from, when you know what He protected you from, you cannot help but SHOUT.

You cannot help but lift your hands. You cannot help but open your mouth. You cannot help but give Him glory. You cannot help but tell somebody. You cannot help but testify. You cannot help but praise Him.

Because your praise is not about impressing people. Your praise is about expressing gratitude. Your praise is not about looking spiritual. Your praise is about being REAL about what God did.

(Pastor Paul wipes sweat, sighs, then wipes again.)

WHEN I STOPPED APOLOGIZING FOR MY PRAISE

I used to apologize for being too loud. Too emotional. Too passionate. Too intense. Too much. But then I realized something. I am not too much. I am GRATEFUL. And grateful people do not whisper. Grateful people SHOUT.

I stopped apologizing for my praise when I realized it was my receipt. My praise is my proof. My praise is my evidence. My praise is my testimony. My praise is my weapon. My praise is my declaration. My praise is my announcement to hell that it LOST.

So if my praise is too loud for you, that is okay. Because it is not for you. It is for HIM. And He deserves EVERY decibel of it.

THE FINAL DECLARATION

So here we are. At the end of this book. At the end of this journey. At the end of these eight chapters. But this is not the end of the story. This is just the end of THIS part of the story.

Because your story is still being written. Your testimony is still unfolding. Your healing is still happening. Your deliverance is still manifesting. Your breakthrough is still coming. Your miracle is still on the way.

And when it comes, when it happens, when it manifests, when it arrives, you are going to do what I did. You are going to open your mouth and say, "THANK YOU, LORD, for ALL You have done for me."

Because that THANK YOU is your PRAISE. And it always will be.

(The organ hums prophetically.)

(Pastor Paul slaps his knee.)

"That was GOD power—NOT mine!"

IMMA WHOOOOOP LIKE HIS STRENGTH LIFTED ME!

(The organ hums powerful.)

Let me close this book the way it deserves to be closed! With a PRAISE! With a SHOUT! With a TESTIMONY! With a DECLARATION!

When I think about EVERYTHING God brought me through! When I think about EVERY storm He carried me through! When I think about EVERY battle He fought for me! When I think about EVERY tear He wiped! When I think about EVERY night He held me! When I think about EVERY morning, He renewed me! When I think about EVERY moment He protected me! My soul goes into PRAISE mode!

Because I should have been dead, but I am ALIVE! I should have been broken, but I am WHOLE! I should have been lost, but I am FOUND! I should have been destroyed, but I am RESTORED! I should have been finished, but I am STILL HERE!

Somebody lift your hands right now because your THANK YOU is your PRAISE! Somebody shout right now because your SURVIVAL is your TESTIMONY! Somebody worship right now because your HEALING is your EVIDENCE! Somebody dance right now because your DELIVERANCE is your PROOF!

And if you KNOW this book is your story too, then lift your voice and say, "THANK YOU, LORD, FOR ALL YOU HAVE DONE FOR ME!"

You walked through fire and did not burn! You walked through water and did not drown! You walked through valleys and did not die! You walked through storms and did not break! You walked through hell and came out WHOLE!

Every time I open my mouth to say THANK YOU, it turns into a PRAISE BREAK! Because I cannot help it! Because I know what He did! Because I know what He saved me from! Because I know what He brought me through!

THANK YOU, LORD! THANK YOU, LORD! THANK YOU, LORD!

This is not the end. This is the BEGINNING. This is your launching pad. This is your new chapter. This is your fresh start. This is your breakthrough moment. This is your testimony season.

Go forward in power! Go forward in confidence! Go forward in faith! Go forward in praise! Go forward in gratitude! Go forward knowing that the same God who kept you THEN is keeping you NOW and will keep you FOREVER!

MY THANK YOU IS MY PRAISE! AND IT ALWAYS WILL BE!

Book Conclusion
This Is Why I Praise

L et me close this book the same way I lived it. With honesty, humor, scars, strength, and Holy Ghost fire.

If you have made it to this conclusion, it means you walked with me through survival, sickness, grief, fear, deliverance, restoration, miracles, protection, mercy, grace, breakthrough, and that long road between "Lord, why now?" and "Lord, thank You."

You read the testimonies. You felt the weight. You saw the journey. You heard the shout. You walked through every "almost" with me. You touched every scar. You visited every valley. You stood in every storm. And now you are here, standing in the sunlight of PRAISE.

Because THAT is how this story ends. Not with sadness. Not with fear. Not with defeat. Not with confusion. Not with shame. Not with regret. This story ends with two things. A survivor and a THANK YOU.

Let me speak to your spirit for a moment. You survived what was designed to break you. You endured what should have left you bitter. You outlived what tried to bury you. You overcame what was meant to destroy you. You rose from things others never recovered from. You are STILL HERE.

Not because you are strong. But because GOD IS FAITHFUL.

And if your life has taught you anything, and mine sure has, it is this. When God keeps you this long, this consistently, this faithfully, this boldly, your THANK YOU becomes your PRAISE.

Gratitude is not an accessory anymore. It is your oxygen. Praise is not a performance. It is your survival language. Worship is not a mood. It is your testimony.

You have seen too much. You have lived too much. You have survived too much. You have cried too much. You have endured too much. You have been healed from too much. You have been forgiven of too much. You have been delivered from too much.

You cannot go back. You cannot stay silent. You cannot pretend you did not see God show up again and again and AGAIN.

This book may be ending, but your PRAISE story is still unfolding. You are stepping into new healing, new joy, new peace, new strength, new power, new favor, new clarity, new purpose, new anointing, new doors, new opportunities, new freedom, new confidence, new miracles, new THANK YOUS.

So as we close this book, lift your hands in your spirit. Lift your head above your past. Lift your faith above your fear. Lift your voice above your circumstances. And declare with authority:

THANK YOU, LORD, FOR ALL YOU HAVE DONE FOR ME.

Because after everything I have lived, everything I have seen, everything I have survived, that THANK YOU IS MY PRAISE. And it always will be.

Final Closing Prayer
Holy Ghost Filled

Father, in the mighty, matchless, miracle-working name of Jesus, we come to the end of this book, but we are nowhere near the end of Your goodness. We pause right here to say: THANK YOU.

Thank You for the chapters You wrote before we had language for them. Thank You for the storms You calmed before we even realized we were drowning. Thank You for the healing You performed when nobody else saw the wound. Thank You for the protection You provided when we were not paying attention. Thank You for the mercy You extended when we did not deserve it. Thank You for the grace that chased us down when we were running from ourselves. Thank You for the peace that settled in places trauma once lived. Thank You for the strength we found in seasons of weakness. Thank You for every breath, every step, every morning, every moment.

God, You have been near us in our sickness, in our sorrow, in our fear, in our failures, in our heartbreak, in our confusion, in our grief, in our doubt, in our silence, in our shadows, in our storms. And still, STILL, You kept us.

So Father, in the name of Jesus: Cover every reader under the shadow of Your wing. Restore every broken place. Heal every hidden wound. Strengthen every weary heart. Silence every lying voice. Break every generational chain. Cancel every hidden assignment of the enemy. Lift every heavy burden. Fill every empty space. Renew every tired mind. Revive every sleeping calling. Refresh every dry spirit. Rebuild every shattered dream.

Replace fear with courage. Replace sorrow with joy. Replace shame with glory. And let Your presence sit on us, rest on us, overflow in us, guide us, protect us, and grow us from this day forward.

Lord, seal this book with power, with purpose, with clarity, with covering, with strength, with joy, and with PRAISE. And let our final declaration be the same one that carried us through every chapter:

THANK YOU, LORD, FOR ALL YOU HAVE DONE FOR ME.

In Jesus' mighty name, Amen. Amen. And AAAAAAMEN.

Author's Closing Blessing
For The Rest Of Your Journey

B efore you close this book, let me lay one more blessing on your spirit.

I pray every dry place in your life gets watered. Every broken place gets healed. Every heavy place gets lifted. Every dark place gets light. Every lonely place gets comfort. Every fearful place gets courage. Every waiting place has a purpose. Every painful place gets peace. Every forgotten place gets revived.

I bless your mind with clarity. Your heart with strength. Your future with direction. Your spirit is refreshed. Your family is protected. Your steps are divinely ordered.

May you walk into the next season of your life with your head held high, your faith strengthened, your joy restored, your purpose ignited, and your praise louder than every attack you survived.

This is not the end. It is the launching pad. Go forward in power. Go forward in confidence. Go forward in God. And remember: He did not keep you this long to leave you now.

With love and blessing,

— **Uncle Paul**

Final Charge
Before You Close This Book

L isten. Do not walk away from these pages as if it were just a cute read. This was not chicken-soup comfort food. This was surgery. This was soul work. This was the Holy Ghost touching your life through words.

So, before you leave, I need you to commit to something. Live louder. Love deeper. Pray bolder. Rest fully. Heal intentionally. And praise God like you mean it.

Your story is not over. Your destiny is not done. Your blessings are not exhausted. Walk out of this book like God just handed you a new chapter because He did.

Praise Break Declaration

I am kept.

I am covered.

I am chosen.

I am protected.

I am strengthened.

I am loved.

I am still here, and that is enough reason to **GIVE GOD PRAISE.**

Reflection Questions
Book Club Guide

1. Which chapter hit you the hardest, and why?

2. What area of your life has God protected that you rarely acknowledge?

3. What "blocked door" in your past was actually a blessing?

4. Where do you need to show more gratitude?

5. What part of your story is ready to be healed?

Reader Response

Share Your Testimony

I want to hear your story. Tell me which chapter spoke to you. Tell me what God healed. Tell me what you survived.

Send your testimony to:

Website: paulstevensmith.com

Social Media: @PaulStevenSmith (all platforms)

Your testimony might help someone else get free.

About The Author

Pastor **Paul Steven Smith**, affectionately known as Uncle Paul, is a writer, pastor, songwriter, abstract artist, storyteller, and survivor from Washington, D.C. His voice blends raw transparency with spiritual depth, cultural humor, and a bold authenticity that resonates across generations.

A shepherd with a comedian's edge, a prophet's insight, and a survivor's testimony, Pastor Paul speaks to hearts that have been bruised, overlooked, forgotten, or weighed down by life.

His message is simple: "You can survive anything, because I survived me."

When he is not writing, Pastor Paul can be found preaching, producing music, encouraging creatives, sipping tea as if it were communion, and reminding folks that healing is holy work.

About The Publisher

KAMB Publishing Group is a creative powerhouse dedicated to elevating Black voices, faith storytellers, and culturally rich narratives that speak to the soul.

We publish books that carry weight, books that tell truth, heal wounds, challenge systems, restore hope, and make readers laugh through their tears.

Our mission: Create stories that change lives and leave a legacy.

Connect With The Author

Website: paulstevensmith.com

YouTube: Uncle Paul's Unpadded Pew

Instagram: @PaulStevenSmith

Facebook: Paul Steven Smith

Other Books By Uncle Paul

Available On Amazon

I Almost Missed My Blessing Because of Fear: When Fear Said No, But God Said Yes!

- It's Time To Move: Stop Talking And Start Moving

- The Prophet's Mantle: Prophetic Word for 2025

Coming Soon

- Put a Pin in It

- The Black Rebuild Project

- Sow, Reap, Repeat

- Get Your Life Together

- Hope Unborn Yet Dead

- This Is Not Shade, It Is Closure

www.ingramcontent.com/pod-product-compliance
Lightning Source LLC
LaVergne TN
LVHW052027080426
835513LV00018B/2210